THE

776

STUPIDEST THINGS

EVER SAID

THE

# 776 STUPIDEST THINGS EVER SAID

**Ross and Kathryn Petras**

Michael O'Mara Books Limited

First published in Great Britain in 1994 by

Michael O'Mara Books Limited
9 Lion Yard
Tremadoc Road
London SW4 7NQ



A CIP catalogue record for this book is available from the British Library

ISBN 1 85479 715 8

Designed and typeset by Florencetype Ltd,
Kewstoke, Avon
Printed and bound in Great Britain by
Cox & Wyman, Reading

10 9 8 7 6 5 4 3 2 1

## Introduction

We've all done it at one time or another – no one is immune to foot-in-mouth disease. People from all walks of life say the wrong thing at the wrong time. Of course, most of us are lucky. When we say something dumb, there's no television camera or newspaper reporter to capture our inadvertent blunders for time immemorial.

But those in the public eye aren't quite so lucky. Their verbal gaffes are recorded in the paper, on air – and now in this book.

This is a collection of the stupidest, most ridiculous, funny, asinine and sometimes frankly frightening quotes in history – anything from misstatements to doublespeak to good old-fashioned idiocy.

*The 776 Stupidest Things Ever Said* is an irreverent look at our pundits, celebrities and politicians and how fallible we all are – them for saying dumb things, us for paying too much attention.

The quotes collected in this book come from a wide range of sources – from newspapers across the country to magazines, from television shows to private collections (or letters). Along the way, we noticed something interesting: like most things, verbal blunders seem to come and go in cycles. While we always relish hearing or reading them, some eras are riper with them than others.

There have been several Golden Ages (of sorts) of the quotable stupidity. An early Golden Age came in the late 1700s and early 1800s, with Anglo-Irish statesman Sir Boyle Roche leading the pack in the misstatement race. One hundred years later, another Golden Age emerged – focusing on gaffes committed in the Houses of Parliament. Then came the early 1920s and the emergence of a wholly American gaffe-watch, caused in part by the tortured syntactical meanderings of President Warren G Harding.

The early 1940s brought another Golden Age. This one, like the attention of the American public in general, centred around Hollywood and the blunders of those connected to the Great American Dream Machine. World War II and the Cold War brought about a lull of sorts in the appreciation of the verbal gaffe. Save for periodic breaks (such as during presidential campaigns), irreverence in general was out.

Then came the late 1960s and a completely new American ethos. The youth revolution swept the nation. Suddenly anything and anyone were fair game. Watergate brought this Golden Age to a peak. And we haven't come off that peak yet. As Yogi Berra said, 'It ain't over till it's over', and it ain't yet.

Just as there are Golden Ages of the verbal gaffe, there are the truly silver-tongued who have more of a knack for the inspired malapropism and verbal blunder than others. That's why we've singled out a few people for special attention: the little-known Sir Boyle Roche, Yogi Berra, Sam Goldwyn, and, more generally, the chief perpetrators of incomprehensible doublespeak – bureaucrats and academics.

But most of this book is a cross section – quotes from people in sports, the arts, the government and the world of business, the famous and the not so famous. Some of the quotes make one think twice about the people in charge of our government, our corporations, our society. Some are clearly mistakes. And others are just plain funny.

And that's really the bottom line. After all, everyone makes mistakes – so why not sit back and enjoy them? Read this book as a celebration of the verbal inanities even the best of us make . . . a celebration of our humanity. It is our hope that it will make even the most tongue-tied of us feel better about ourselves. If the best and the brightest can do it and go on to become presidents, kings and generals, why not me?

## Accidents

. . . hazards are one of the main causes of accidents.

*From the US Occupational Safety and Health Administration's booklet,* Safety with Beef Cattle

## Actuality

Things are more like they are now than they have ever been.

*President Gerald Ford*

## Adages, Modern Interpretations of

As Duke Ellington once said, 'The Battle of Waterloo was won on the playing fields of Elkton.'

*Babe Ruth on a radio show, garbling the adage by the Duke of Wellington that Waterloo was won on the playing fields of Eton*

## Addresses

If at any time I change my address when I notify you I hope you will be so kind as to change also.

*Letter from a reader renewing his subscription, received by the business manager of* Motor News

## Adoptions, Reasons Why You May Be Excluded from

It would seem from the interviews and reports that both of you have had few, if any, negative experiences when children yourselves, and also seem to enjoy a marital experience where rows and arguments have no place. Under the circumstances, [adopted children would not have sufficient exposure to] negative experiences.

*Letter from the Lancashire (UK) Social Services Department, on why foster parents Harry and Esther Hough were not qualified to adopt as they 'exuded excessive harmony', although they had already raised over forty foster children from birth to aged eight*

## Advice

Life its own self, as Dan Jenkins said. Life its own self. Figure that one out, Norm. But what it means is, I have a lot more to learn from President Reagan.

*George Bush, at the beginning of his presidency, when asked whether he was getting advice from his predecessor*

Don't cut off your nose yourself.

*Casey Stengel*

## Age

Bruce Sutter has been around for a while and he's pretty old. He's thirty-five years old. That will give you some idea of how old he is.

*Ron Fairly, San Francisco Giants broadcaster*

## Agreeing

And what is more, I agree with everything I have just said.

*Attributed to Piet Koornhoff, South African cabinet minister, Ambassador to United States*

## Agreements

If I entered into an agreement with that man, I would be sticking my head in a moose.

*Attributed to movie mogul, Samuel Goldwyn*

## Air Fares, Free

Gifts are positively corruptive . . . [Free air fares] are harmless, or at least only potentially corruptive.

*Lee Wilbur, staff aide on the House Appropriations Transportation sub-committee, explaining why it was okay for him to accept a free (first-class) round trip flight to Spain*

## Alliteration, Excessive

Progression is not proclamation nor palaver. It is not pretence nor play on prejudice. It is not of personal pronouns, nor perennial pronouncement. It is not the perturbation of a people passion-wrought, nor a promise proposed.

*President Warren G Harding*

## Ambassadors

This is the man who was not only the president of the National Council of Shopping Centers, but the International Council of Shopping Centers in 1986, and travelled around the world.

*Senator Rudy Boschwitz of Minnesota in his recommendation for the appointment of Melvin F Sembler to the post of ambassador to Australia, as quoted in* Spy, *May 1990. Sembler was appointed and confirmed shortly thereafter*

I understand it's a nice lifestyle. I love golf, and I understand they have a lot of nice golf courses.

*Chic Hecht, former senator from Nevada, explaining why he would like to be appointed ambassador to the Bahamas (Note: Shortly after saying this, Hecht did become ambassador to the Bahamas)*

## American Greatness

That's part of American greatness, is discrimination. Yes, sir. Inequality, I think, breeds freedom and gives a man opportunity.

*Lester Maddox, ex-governor of Georgia*

## AMERICANS



Maybe we should not have humoured them . . . [when they asked to live on reservations]. Maybe we should have said, 'No, come join us. Be citizens along with the rest of us.'

*President Ronald Reagan during a trip to Moscow, when a student asked him about US treatment of Native Americans*

I don't feel we did wrong in taking this great country away from them. There were great numbers of people who needed new land, and the Indians were selfishly trying to keep it for themselves.

*John Wayne, actor who played mostly cowboys in the movies*

Get some more from the reservoir.

*Supposedly said by movie mogul, Samuel Goldwyn after being told that the Western film he was working on required more Native American extras*

Wherever I have gone in this country, I have found Americans.

*Alf Landon (in America), during a speech in his presidential campaign against FDR*

## ANIMALS

I believe that mink are raised for being turned into fur coats and if we didn't wear fur coats those little animals would never have been born. So is it better not to have been born or to have been turned into a fur coat? I don't know.

*Barbi Benton, ex-*Playboy *bunny turned actress*

## Answers

I think we're on the road to coming up with answers that I don't think any of us in total feel we have the answers to.

*Kim Anderson, mayor of Naples, Florida*

My position on Vietnam is very simple. And I feel this way. I haven't spoken on it because I haven't felt there was any major contribution that I had to make at the time. I think that our concepts as a nation and that our actions have not kept pace with the changing conditions, and therefore our actions are not completely relevant today to the realities of the magnitude and the complexity of the problems that we face in this conflict.

*Nelson Rockefeller, governor of New York, when asked in a press conference for his position on the Vietnam War. When a reporter followed up with a question asking what he meant, Rockefeller answered, 'Just what I said.'*

## Appreciation

You're a parasite for sore eyes.

*Attributed to actor/director, Gregory Ratoff*

## ART

Rembrandt is not to be compared in the painting of character with our extraordinarily gifted artist, Mr Rippingdale.

*John Hunt, nineteenth-century art critic*

Culture is necessary, but it must be alive and not too much of it.

*Virginia Gayda, official in Fascist Italy*

When it comes to ruining a painting, he's an artist.

*Movie mogul, Samuel Goldwyn, on an abstract artist*

## ASSIMILATION

My fellow astronauts . . .

*Vice-President Dan Quayle, beginning a speech at an* Apollo 11 *anniversary celebration*

## ATHLETES

Arnie [Palmer], usually a great putter, seems to be having trouble with his long putt. However he has no trouble dropping his shorts.

*Golf broadcaster on the air during a tournament*

## AUSTRALIA HOUSE

And for those of you who don't know Australia House, it's a beautiful Victorian building . . . the first brick was laid in 1913 by King George V.

*Rolf Harris*

## Bad Deals

My dear Mr Wallis, just read Sea Wolf. You told me in your office that it would be a 50-50 part (the role of Leach). I am sorry to say it is just the opposite.

*George Raft, actor, in wire to Hal Wallis, producer*

## Baseball

Half this game is ninety per cent mental.

*Danny Ozark, manager of the Philadelphia Phillies*

Would the fans along the outfield please remove their clothes?

*Tex Rikards, public address announcer at Ebbets Field, Brooklyn, New York, after fans had used the top of the outfield fence for their coats*

## Beards

I've been travelling so much, I haven't had time to grow it.

*Bob Horner, Atlanta Braves third baseman, on why he hadn't grown a beard*

## Being in Two Places at One Time

No refreshments shall be supplied to any member after the above named hours, and none shall be supplied for consumption off the club premises except to a member on the premises at the time.

*By-law in a private social club rulebook*

## Being Shot Through the Right Temple

Isn't it a blessing of God it didn't hit him in the eye?

*An elderly woman, when she and two others found a dead robber on the road, shot through the right temple*

## Being There

Well, sir, I met you this morning, but you did not come; however, I'm determined to meet you tomorrow morning, whether you come or not.

*A challenger to a man who didn't show up for a scheduled duel, reported by nineteenth-century Writer J C Percy*

## Believability

Anything that man says you've got to take with a dose of salts.

*Movie mogul, Samuel Goldwyn*

## Birds, Communist

The lark is exclusively a Soviet bird. The lark does not like the other countries, and lets its harmonious song be heard only over the fields made fertile by the collective labour of the citizens of the happy land of the Soviets.

*From a novel by the not so noted Soviet novelist DBleiman*

## Birds, Strange Abilities of

A man could not be in two places at the same time unless he were a bird.

*Sir Boyle Roche, eighteenth-century MP from Tralee*

## Birth

I called the doctor, and he told me that the contraptions were an hour apart.

*Mackey Sasser, New York Mets catcher, on his wife's labour*

## Blacks versus Whites

It is just not accurate to believe that blacks were confined somehow to the lowest-paying jobs; rather, there was some tendency for blacks to be congregated in certain units which had a variety of characteristics including, in some instances, a somewhat lower average pay than some units where there might be a heavy concentration of white employees.

*Ben Fisher, special assistant to the president of United Steelworkers of America, in* New Times

## Blame

We have only one person to blame, and that's each other.

*Barry Beck, New York Ranger, on who started a brawl during the National Hockey League's Stanley Cup play-offs*

## Blockbusters

It will create an excitement that will sweep the country like wild-flowers.

*Movie mogul, Samuel Goldwyn*

This will start with a bang in Hollywood and degenerate throughout the whole world.

*Movie mogul, Samuel Goldwyn*

## Bombing

They [the bombs] are aimed exclusively at military targets. . . Unfortunately there are some civilians around these targets.

*Dwight D Eisenhower, former President and general, standing up for the way the United States was handling bombing in North Vietnam*

Everybody should rise up and say, 'Thank you, Mr President, for bombing Haiphong.'

*Martha Mitchell, wife of Attorney General John Mitchell, addressing a Republican Women's Conference*

You always write it's bombing, bombing, bombing. It's not bombing, it's air support.

*US Air Force Colonel David Opfer, air attaché in Cambodia, complaining to reporters about their coverage of the Vietnam War*

## Bonuses, Reason for Giving Over $195 Million

If we didn't have bonuses, we wouldn't have had anybody working for us.

*Drexel Burnham Lambert spokesperson, explaining why the company gave over $195 million in bonuses just before it filed for bankruptcy*

## Books

[Does] the published book contain the unpublished part?

*James H Campbell, King's Counsel, to a witness in Britain's Times Book Club case in the early 1990s*

## Book Titles

*Correctly English in 100 Days*

*Title from an East Asian book*

## Bosses, Admiration of

I first saw [President Reagan] as a foot, highly polished brown cordovan wagging merrily on a hassock. I spied it through the door. It was a beautiful foot, sleek. Such casual elegance and clean lines! But not a big foot, not formidable, maybe a little . . . frail. I imagined cradling it in my arms, protecting it from unsmooth roads.

*Peggy Noonan, speechwriter for the Reagan administration, in her memoirs*

## Bottles

Every pint bottle should contain a quart.

*Sir Boyle Roche, eighteenth-century MP from Tralee and pre-eminent word mangler, on government regulation*

## Bread and Butter

If you let that sort of thing go on, your bread and butter will be cut right out from under your feet.

*Ernest Bevin, British Foreign Minister, 1945–1951*

## Bribes

I didn't want it to be too big. It would have made it look like we bought the decision.

*Jake Jacobsen, former Associated Milk Producers lawyer, testifying to a federal jury on the $10,000 he gave to former Treasury Secretary John Connally for help on milk prices*

I would categorize them more as gifts.

*Aerospace manufacturer Lockheed's chief operations officer, trying to explain about the $7 million paid to government officials from Holland and to an influential Japanese right-winger*

I don't see anything unusual about it.

*Edwin Edwards, Louisiana governor, in 1976, after admitting that his wife accepted $10,000 from a Korean businessman with ties to the South Korean CIA*

## Broadcasting

We are experiencing audio technicalities.

*Ralph Kiner, announcer for the New York Mets*

## Bureaucracy

Due to an administrative error, the original of the attached letter was forwarded to you. A new original has been accomplished and forwarded to AAC/JA (Alaskan Air Command, Judge Advocate office). Please place this carbon copy in your files and destroy the original.

*A memo from the Alaska Air Command, February 1973*

## Burial

It is deplorable to think of a parish where there are 30,000 people living without a Christian burial.

*Clergyman fund-raising for a graveyard, as reported in the* Spectator, *mid-80s*

I suppose you think that on our board half the directors do the work and the other half do nothing. As a matter of fact, gentlemen, the reverse is the case.

*A chairman of the board of a prominent company defending his fellow directors*

I'll tell you, it's Big Business. If there is one word to describe Atlantic City, it's Big Business. Or two words – Big Business.

*Donald Trump, real estate tycoon, looking down on Atlantic City from his helicopter, as quoted in a 1989* Time

## Campaign promises

[I want to] make sure everybody who has a job wants a job.

*George Bush, during his first campaign for the presidency*

## Capability

Mike Andrews's limits are limitless.

*Danny Ozark, Philadelphia Phillies' manager, about one of his players*

## Capital Punishment

Capital punishment is our society's recognition of the sanctity of human life.

*Orrin Hatch, Republican senator from Utah, explaining his support of the death penalty*

## Cartoon Characters

While you are away, movie stars are taking your women. Robert Redford is dating your girlfriend, Tom Selleck is kissing your lady, Bart Simpson is making love to your wife.

*Baghdad Betty, Iraqi radio announcer, to Gulf War troops*

## Casting

For this part of a lady, somebody that's couth.

*Movie mogul, Samuel Goldwyn*

## Celebrity

[I introduce to you the Reverend Father McFadden] known all over the world, and other places besides.

*Introduction in Parliament, nineteenth century*

## Censorship

We do not have censorship. What we have is a limitation on what newspapers can report.

*Louis Nel, former Deputy Minister of Information for South Africa*

Without censorship, things can get terribly confused in the public mind.

*General William Westmoreland on why the media should be muzzled in wartime*

## Character Judgments

Your commitment and compassion, your humanitarian principles and your interest in protecting individual liberty and freedom have made an outstanding contribution to furthering the cause of human dignity.

*Joseph Califano, Jr, then Secretary of Health, Education and Welfare, in a letter of reverence for cult leader and mass murderer Jim Jones*

## Chickens

Chickens, like two-edged swords, ofttimes come home to roost.

*Newspaper editor in Wisconsin*

## Children

So Carol, you're a housewife and mother. And have you got any children?

*Michael Barrymore*

## Childhood Innocence

The boys never meant any harm against the girls. They just meant to rape.

*Joyce Kithira, deputy principal of a Kenyan boarding school, commenting on a raid of a girls' dormitory by a gang of boys who raped seventy-one girls and killed nineteen*

## China

China is a big country, inhabited by many Chinese.

*Charles de Gaulle, French President*

## Chinese Sayings

Hey, listen. I'm a member of the NRA. You're hurting my feelings, as they say in China.

*President George Bush, explaining why he didn't come out strongly against violence against women in an address to the National Rifle Association*

## Chivalry

Chivalry is only reasonably dead.

*George Bush, offering a chair to a woman*

## Civil Rights

We may be finding that in some blacks when [the carotid choke hold] is applied, the veins or arteries do not open up like . . . normal people.

*Daryl Gates, Los Angeles police chief, discussing a department investigation he said he had instituted in an effort to explain why a high percentage of blacks died as a result of police officers using the choke hold on them*

I'm not against the blacks and a lot of the good blacks will attest to that.

*Evan Mecham, then governor of Arizona*

I can't get over saying 'coloured'. I said it all my life. All the Negroes seem to resent it and I don't know why.

*Martha Mitchell, wife of Attorney General John Mitchell*

Booker T Washington, the great black nigger . . . uh . . . educator . . . uh . . . excuse me for making that . . . the great black educator . . . the Negro educator.

*Reagan Brown, Texas agriculture commissioner, addressing agriculture professors and attempting to refer to the accomplishments of Booker T Washington*

This country needs a spear chucker, and I think we've got him up on this podium.

*Eugene Dorff, mayor of Kenosha, Wisconsin, introducing presidential candidate, Jesse Jackson. He said later he had intended to say 'straight shooter', but slipped*

## CLARIFICATION

[That report was] . . . a wholly garbled version of what never took place.

*Augustine Birrel, Chief Secretary for Ireland, 1907–1916, whose inability to stop the plotting that led to the Easter Rebellion forced him to retire*

This is the operative statement. The others are inoperative.

*Ron Ziegler, press secretary to President Richard Nixon*

I never said I had no idea about most of the things you said I said I had no idea about.

*Elliot Abrams, Assistant Secretary of State, clarifying himself before a 1987 congressional hearing*

That was consciously ambiguous in the sense that any terrorist government or terrorist movement that is contemplating such actions I think knows clearly what we are speaking of.

*Alexander Haig, then Secretary of State, when asked by a reporter to make a statement clearer*

I stand by all the misstatements.

*Dan Quayle, then vice-presidential candidate, defending himself against criticism for making verbal gaffes*

## ON CLARITY

JOHN SUNUNU (then governor of New Hampshire): You're telling us that the reason things are so bad is that they are so good, and they will get better as soon as they get worse?

JAMES A BAKER (then Secretary of the Treasury): You got it.

The Gang of Four (and Lin Piao) were using an ultra-Left stance as a cover for a factional attempt to seize power. If the Gang of Four are incorrectly labelled leftists or ultra-'leftists', this broadens the attack to include anyone who made honest 'Left' errors. This would play into the hands of the Right in a situation where an evaluation of the positive and negative results of the Cultural Revolution could present an opportunity for rightist attacks on the real positive breakthroughs that have occurred. This is the significance of the correct evaluation of the Gang of Four that has been made – that they were, in essence, ultra-rightists and not leftists.

*Pat and Roger Howard, from the Institute of Foreign Languages, Canton, China, in 1977 issue of the Maoist newspaper, the* Guardian

## On Clear Thinking

An agency subject to the provisions of the Federal Reports Act may enter into an arrangement with an organization not subject to the Act whereby the organization not subject to the Act collects information on behalf of the agency subject to the Act. The reverse also occurs.

*A memo from the Office of Management and Budget (OMB)*

We offer the party as a big tent. How we do that within the platform, the preamble to the platform, or whatnot, that remains to be seen. But that message will have to be articulated with great clarity.

*Vice-President Dan Quayle (This comment was awarded the British Golden Bull award)*

## Coal-miners

We shall have no coal industry if the miners are driven into the ground.

*Claire Brooks*

## Comebacks

We on this side of the House are not such fools as we look.

*House member overheard retorting to taunts*

## Comedy

Our comedies are not to be laughed at.

*Movie mogul, Samuel Goldwyn*

## Commies

[The Soviet Union is using] every device of propaganda in an effort to hinder the rebuilding of America's defenses and force a hasty resumption of arms negotiations.

*Eugene Rostow, director of the US Arms Control and Disarmament Agency, in the* Philadelphia Inquirer

## Communications

The communication and exchange of ideas on administrative policy matters is encouraged and maintained to optimize the use, mix and cost and administrative inputs in program results.

*Treasury Board of Canada memo*

## Communism

In every country the Communists have taken over, the first thing they do is outlaw cockfighting.

*John Monks, Oklahoma state representative, arguing against a bill that would make cockfighting illegal in the state*

I did not want to tire the population, because otherwise it would have stayed up too late.

*Nicolae Ceausescu, Romanian dictator, explaining why television viewing was restricted to only two hours a night. He neglected to add that electricity was usually cut off during night hours due to his own economic mismanagement.*

Gerald Ford was a Communist.

*Ronald Reagan in a speech. He later indicated he meant to say 'Congressman'*

## Compliments

Elderly woman (on a hot day in St Petersburg, Florida): Good afternoon, Mr Berra. My, you look mighty cool today.

Yogi Berra: Thank you, ma'am. You don't look so hot yourself.

## Congress

[I support efforts] to limit the terms of members of Congress, especially members of the House and members of the Senate.

*Vice-President Dan Quayle*

Let me tell you that tolerance is one thing, intolerance another. To be a person intolerant of another person's right to have different views is my idea of tolerance, that is, until that person endeavours to make a public issue of his views.

*Congressman Albert Johnson of Washington, Chairman of the House Committee of Immigration*

## Constitution

We need to take a look at it and maybe from time to time we should curtail some of those rights.

*LeRoy Martin, Chicago Police superintendent*

## Consumer Protection

Honest businessmen should be protected from the unscrupulous consumer.

*Lester Maddox, then governor of Georgia, on why Georgia should not create a consumer protection agency*

## Contortions

Why should Irishmen stand with their arms folded and their hands in their pockets when England called for aid?

*Sir Thomas Myles, speaking at a meeting in Dublin in 1902, about the Boer War*

## Contracts

A verbal contract isn't worth the paper it's written on.

*Movie mogul, Samuel Goldwyn*

## Conviction

If Governor Fields is right, I am going to stand by him because he is right. If he is wrong, I am going to stand by him because he is a Democrat.

*Senator Augustus Owsley Stanley (D-Ken) during the 1920s*

Young people, do not be led astray by the theory of voting for the man and not for the party. Vote the straight Republican ticket regardless of the qualifications of the candidate for office.

*C J Travis, Supreme Court of Indiana in the 1920s*

## Cooking

The female teachers were instructed in cooking. They had, in fact, to go through the process of cooking themselves in turn.

*In the annual report of the Commissioners of National Education in Ireland*

## Corporate Etiquette

Avoid saying 'hello'. This elsewhere pleasant and familiar greeting is out of place in the world of business.

*Instructions of Morgan Guaranty Trust Company to New York employees*

## Counting

The interests of the employers and the employed are the same nine times out of ten – I will even say ninety-nine times out of ten.

*Lord Curzon, British statesman and Viceroy of India from 1898 to 1905, Oxford University Chancellor and Foreign Secretary from 1919 to 1924*

## Covert Operation

The word is not covert, it's overt. Covert means you're out in the open. Overt is what I did. [Which means] I was under cover.

*Chic Hecht, Nevada senator, talking about his eighteen years of participation in covert operations as an army intelligence officer*

## Cover-ups

No one in the White House staff, no one in this administration, presently employed, was involved in this very bizarre incident . . . What really hurts in matters of this sort is not the fact that they occur, because over-zealous people in campaigns do things that are wrong. What really hurts is if you try to cover it up.

*President Nixon, at the beginning of the Watergate affair*

That is, because of, because of our, that is, we are attempting, the position is to without information and to cover up – that is totally true – you could say it is totally untrue.

*President Richard Nixon, from 1973 White House transcripts, discussing whether or not to hide evidence concerning the Watergate break-in*

## Cows

A cow may be drained dry; and if the chancellors of the exchequer persist in meeting every deficiency that occurs by taxing the brewing and distilling industries, they will inevitably kill the cow that lays the golden milk.

*Sir Frederick Milner, MP, circa 1900*

The best way to pass a cow on the road when cycling is to keep behind it.

*R J Mecredy, writer and publisher of cycling magazines in a column offering advice on country bicycling to novices*

## Cramming

We must have a nation of all-Americans. We must expel those who cannot recite the Constitution of the United States and Lincoln's Gettysburg Address.

*Ex-Iowa Governor, William Harding*

## Crime

If crime were down 100 per cent, it would still be fifty times higher than it should be.

*Councilman John Bowman, commenting on the high crime in Washington, DC*

The streets are safe in Philadelphia, it's only the people who make them unsafe.

*Frank Rizzo, ex-police chief and Mayor of Philadelphia*

The more killing and homicides you have, the more havoc it prevents.

*Richard M Daley, Mayor of Chicago, commenting on the rise of crime in his city*

Outside of the killings, [Washington] has one of the lowest crime rates in the country.

*Mayor Marion Barry, Washington DC*

## Crime Prevention

When anyone is held up, he shall immediately telephone the details to a telephone operator. She will plug in every phone in the city and relate the details of the hold-up. Near every telephone a shotgun is to be kept hanging on the wall. When the story of the hold-up is spread through the phones, every citizen will seize his shotgun and rush to the street. All whistles will blow and at this signal all traffic, including pedestrians, will halt. Anyone, besides Law offices, who moves will be shot.

*Revd George W Durham, Quindaro Methodist Church of Kansas City, on how to stop crime in Kansas City, as quoted in the* Kansas City Journal, *1925*

## Criticism

That lowdown scoundrel deserves to be kicked to death by a jackass – and I'm just the one to do it.

*A congressional candidate in Texas, reported by Massachusetts State Senator John F Parker*

## Criticism

It rolls off my back like a duck.

*Movie mogul, Samuel Goldwyn*

## Cutting the Budget

When there is duplicity in personnel, it must be eliminated. Teachers who are of retirement age should be urged to do so.

*Hoboken, New Jersey, city councilman in a political ad-letter*

## Sir Boyle Roche and 'Irish Bulls'

Sir Boyle Roche was born with his foot in his mouth – and he kept it there.

He was the spiritual grandfather of such masters as Yogi Berra and Sam Goldwyn, the true father of the verbal blunder and malapropism, called in his day and up through the early 1900s the 'Irish Bull'.

*The term 'bull' itself came from the blunderings of a certain Obadiah Bull, an Irish lawyer in London. Unfortunately, most of his errors are lost to history, but Sir Boyle is still vigorously alive, thanks to such collectors as G R Neilson in 1898 and James C Percy in 1915.*

*Sir Boyle Roche was a forceful personality with a vigorous, sometimes florid way of mixing metaphors and everything else. For example, in the middle of an impassioned speech to the House of Commons on the French Revolution, he said:*

'If those Gallican villains should invade us, sir ... perhaps the murderous martial law men would break in, cut us into joints, and throw our bleeding heads on the table to stare us in the face.'

Needless to say, like Elvis, he became 'a living legend in his own time', and probably a good number of his blunders were not made by him, but merely attributed to him.

*As Sir Boyle himself said:*

'Half the lies our opponents tell about us are not true.'

*A few of Sir Boyle's best*

[They are] living from hand-to-mouth like the birds of the air. (describing the poverty of Irish farmers)

Little children who could neither walk nor talk were running about in the streets cursing their Maker. (in a speech about the poor conditions of the times)

All along the untrodden paths of the future, I can see the footprints of an unseen hand.

While I write this letter, I have a pistol in one hand and a sword in the other.

The farmers of Ireland ought to dispense with the use of wooden gates, and put up cast-iron ones instead, as the latter would last forever and in the end could be utilized for making horse-shoes.

If you ever come within a mile of our house, will you stop there all night? (in a letter to a friend)

Many thousands of them were destitute of even the goods they possessed.

I answer in the affirmative with an emphatic, 'No.'

Sir, I would anchor a frigate off each bank of the river, with strict orders not to stir; and so, by cruising up and down, put a stop to smuggling. (his suggestion for halting smuggling on the Shannon River)

Anybody who wishes to diminish the brotherly affection of the two sister countries is an enemy to both nations. (speaking about the union between Britain and Ireland)

Single misfortunes never come alone, and the greatest of all national calamities is generally followed by one greater.

The cup of our trouble is running over, but, alas, is not yet full.

## De-Sexed Language

Senate Agriculture Chairman, Jesse Helms: Attaboy, Senator! Atta, uh, girl . . . person . . . what are you anyway?

Representative, Paula Hawkins (R-Fla): I'm not a person, I'm a lady!

[Personhole] is not an acceptable de-sexed word.

*Shirley Dean, councilperson from the Berkeley, California, City Council, explaining why the council changed the wording in a sewer equipment request back to manhole cover*

## Death

Before the Home Rule Bill is enforced, Asquith will have to walk over many dead bodies – his own included.

*From a 1914 letter written by an Ulster Unionist about Herbert Henry Asquith, British Prime Minister, who introduced a bill to grant Ireland self-rule*

It is what we must all come to if we only live long enough.

*Reported by David Garrick, eighteenth-century English actor, manager and dramatist*

My friends, I desire that you will make a post-mortem examination of me, and find out what ails me; for really I am dying to know what my disease is myself.

*James Smithson, benefactor of the Smithsonian Institution, on his deathbed*

Your medical assistance is cancelled beginning 24/9/84 because of your death.

*Letter from the Iowa Department of Human Services*

Beginning in February 1976 your assistance benefits will be discontinued . . . Reason: it has been reported to our office that you expired on 1 January 1976.

*Illinois Department of Public Aid*

Beware! To touch these wires is instant death. Anyone found doing so will be prosecuted.

*On a sign at a railroad station*

Well, that kind of puts a damper on even a Yankee win.

*Yankee broadcaster Phil Rizzuto, during a game in which news reached him that Pope Paul had died*

We just lost a pope, which is very sad, and now we lost to the Yankees, which is also very sad.

*Humberto Cardinal Medeiros, discussing the loss of the Boston Red Sox to the Yankees during play-offs*

At the next election, we have got to give the third, and I hope the last, death-blow to Home Rule.

*Edward Henry Stanley, 15th Earl of Derby, then leader of the Liberal Unionists in the House of Lords during the debate on Irish Home Rule*

When an Englishman wants to get married, to whom does he go? To the clergy. When he wants to get his child baptized, to whom does he go? To the clergy. When he wants to get buried, to whom does he go?

*William E Gladstone, leader of the Liberal Party of England and Prime Minister, in a speech extolling the clergy*

Where would Christianity be if Jesus got eight to fifteen years, with time off for good behaviour?

*New York State Senator, James H Donovan, on capital punishment*

## Decision-making

If you leave this question to us for three years, we will settle it tomorrow morning.

*Irish MP during a nineteenth-century debate*

## Definitions

Democracy: A government of the masses ... Results in mobocracy. Attitude towards property is communistic – negating property rights ... Result is demogogism, license, agitation, discontent, anarchy.

*From a US Army Training Manual dated 1928*

We found the term 'killing' too broad.

*State Department spokesperson on why the word 'killing' was replaced with 'unlawful or arbitrary deprivation of life' in its human rights reports for 1984–5*

We may, of course, define emotions as the autopoetic immune system the autopoetic psychic system; but again: is this emotionally adequate?

*Niklas Luhman, in his article 'The Individuality of the Individual', in* Reconstructing Individualism

## Dioxin

[Exposure to dioxin is] usually not disabling but may be fatal.

*Dow Chemical Company report, as quoted in* The Progressive

## Diplomacy

Anything concerning the ambassador's swimming pool must be referred to as water storage tank not as *swimming pool.*

*Internal State Department memo, US Embassy, Vientiane, Laos*

You know, your nose looks just like Danny Thomas's.

*President Ronald Reagan to the Lebanese Foreign Minister, during a briefing on the realities of the Middle-East conflict*

Some of them have marvellous minds, those black people over there.

*Director of the United States Information Agency, Charles Z Wick, after a 1983 trip to Africa*

Why thresh old straw or beat an old bag of bones?

*Senator Everett Dirksen of Illinois, annoyed with attacks against Clare Boothe Luce and her nomination to be ambassador to Brazil, during a Senate debate. He quickly added that 'old bag of bones' was not a reference to Luce*

Look, I'm going to tell you something, hon. You've crossed and uncrossed your legs twice and one time you showed me something I shouldn't see. Now am I going to complain that you're loosey-goosey or you got no class?

*US Ambassador-nominee to Italy, Pete Secchia, to a female reporter from the Detroit News. He was later confirmed as Ambassador to Italy*

This is a great day for France!

*President Richard Nixon while attending Charles De Gaulle's funeral*

I didn't know the guy was a nigger.

*Senator James Eastland to his aide after welcoming Egyptian President Anwar Sadat, reported in* New Times

German President Heinrich Lubke, on the tarmac in his role as official greeter in 1962, trying to say 'How are you?': Who are you?

PRESIDENT OF INDIA: I am the President of India.

The only thing I regret is that your stay is not shorter.

*Lord Aberdeen, trying to make a good impression while being visited by the colonial Premier to Ireland in the autumn of 1911*

If I never get to Mexico again, it wouldn't bother me. I don't like the food or the climate.

*Dan R Eddy, Jr, member of Texas Good Neighbor Commission, a state agency charged with promoting Texas–Mexico good relations*

The treaty has to be concocted to satisfy all tastes. One prepares the seafood, the meat, the chicken and the rice, but they are just an assortment of separate dishes until they are blended into perfect unity, and the result is paella – or a treaty for all.

*Bernardo Zuleta, Secretary General of the United Nations Law of the Sea Conference*

## Directions

Separate together in a bunch. [And don't] stand around so much in little bundles.

*Director Michael Curtiz to movie extras*

Every move helter . . . and skelter.

*Movie mogul, Samuel Goldwyn*

## Disasters

This is the worst disaster in California since I was elected.

*California Governor Pat Brown, discussing a local flood*

## DISNEY

With the Euro-Disney soon to be built just across the Channel, British Theme Parks will just seem Mickey Mouse affairs.

*Neil Walker*

## DISTINGUISHING CHARACTERISTICS

. . . the deceased had an impediment in his speech.

*Mayor in Estremadura province, Portugal, giving tips while announcing a search for a drowned man*

## DIVERSITY

We have every mixture you can have. I have a black, I had a woman, two Jews and a cripple.

*James Watt, Secretary of the Interior, referring to an advisory group in his agency*

## DIVINE CALLINGS

It's not listed in the Bible, but my spiritual gift, my specific calling from God, is to be a television talk-show host.

*James Bakker, televangelist. He said this before he was indicted*

## DOGS

Sir, it requires only a spark to let slip the dogs of war.

*Lord Hartington, Duke of Devonshire, leader of the Liberal Unionists, during a debate on the critical state of relations between Russia and Turkey in 1877*

## Drafting for the Army

I did what any normal person would do at that age. You call home. You call home to mother and father and say, 'I'd like to get into the National Guard.'

*Dan Quayle, then Republican vice-presidential candidate, defending his National Guard service during the Vietnam War*

## Dualism

None but himself can be his parallel.

*Louis Theobald, eighteenth-century English critic, famous collator of Shakespeare, and author of* The Double Falsehood

## Drugs

Now, like, I'm President. It would be pretty hard for some drug guy to come into the White House and start offering it up, you know? . . . I bet if they did, I hope I would say, 'Hey, get lost. We don't want any of that.'

*President Bush, talking about drug abuse to a group of students*

. . . casual drug users ought to be taken out and shot.

*Daryl Gates, Los Angeles police chief, telling the Senate Judiciary Committee what should be done with casual users of marijuana and cocaine*

## EARTH

The government is not doing enough about cleaning up the environment. This is a great planet.

*Contestant for Mr New Jersey Male, when asked what he would do with a million dollars.*

## ECONOMICS

In all likelihood, world inflation is over.

*Managing Director of the International Monetary Fund in 1959*

## ECONOMISTS

There may be a recession in stock prices, but not anything in the nature of a crash.

*Irving Fisher, economist, six weeks before the 1929 crash*

Stock prices have reached what looks like a permanently high plateau.

*Irving Fisher, economist, in a speech made nine days before the 1929 crash*

The depression has ended . . . In July, up we go.

*Dr Julius Klein, Assistant Secretary of Commerce, in a speech given on 9 June 1931. The following year, 1932, is generally considered the worst in the Depression*

## EDUCATION

There were allegations a number of students at schools in Brooklyn may have been involved in having some knowledge, particularly about social studies and possibly English.

*Samuel Polatnick, Executive Director of the Board of Education's Division of High Schools (1975)*

## ELECTIONS

Minnesota voters played a major role in the victory of that state's gubernatorial primary elections yesterday.

*National Rifle Association press release*

## ELECTRIC CHAIR

Folks read about the electric chair, they hear about it – but those folks with criminal minds don't care about the law. But if they see that chair moving down the highway, it may save a life.

*Georgia State Senator, Ronnie Walker, on the need for a travelling electric chair that would traverse the state for county executions*

## Eloquence

[President Carter] speaks loudly and carries a fly spotter, a fly swasher – it's been a long day.

*President Gerald Ford, in a speech during the 1976 presidential campaign*

## Emphasis

[I will] put down my foot with a strong hand.

*Overheard at a shareholders' meeting*

## Emptiness

In a few weeks it had been found out that this promise was full of emptiness.

*W Brodrick, Lord Midleton, British statesman who served in various posts including Secretary of State for War in India in the early 1900s*

## English

If English was good enough for Jesus Christ, it's good enough for me.

*A congressman to Dr David Edwards, head of the Joint National Committee on Language, about the necessity for a commercial nation to be multilingual*

Every nation must have its own traditional language as a primary language, which if it was not English is not likely to be.

*George C McGhee, 'English – Best Hope for a World Language'* Saturday Review/World

## Entertainment

It's dull from beginning to end. But it's loaded with entertainment.

*Michael Curtiz, a Hollywood director, on a musical*

## Environment

It's time to stand the history of wetlands destruction on its head.

*George Bush, discussing wetlands protection with the group Ducks Unlimited*

## Epitaphs

Here lies Captain Ernest Bloomfield. Accidentally shot by his orderly, 2 March 1879. Well done, good and faithful servant.

*Grave inscription of British soldier, in Northwest Frontier of modern-day Pakistan*

## Equal Pay

The College's Affirmative Action Policy and the policy of non-discrimination which assure equal employment opportunity and access to programmes are based on the following state and federal laws, and executive orders:

. . . 12) Equal Pay Act of 1963 (requires equal sex for equal work)

*Evergreen State College handbook, reported in* The Chronicle of Higher Education

## Equal Rights

Equal rights were created for everyone.

*Contestant in the 1990 Mr New Jersey Male pageant*

Human beings are not animals, and I do not want to see sex and sexual differences treated as casually and amorally as dogs and other beasts treat them. I believe this could happen under the ERA.

*Ronald Reagan, speaking against the Equal Rights Amendment*

## Ethics

I've got 423 dairy farmers in my district, and I've got to rise above principles.

*Tennessee State Representative, John Bragg, on why he was for [fair trade pricing] price controls on milk but against it for spirits*

## Etiquette

The chairs in the cabin are for the ladies. Gentlemen are not to make use of them till the ladies are seated.

*Instructions posted in a river cruise ship, Suir River, Ireland*

## Eulogies

A great Irishman has passed away. God grant that as many great, and who wisely love their country, may follow him.

The Times, *as reported in* Handy-Book of Literary Curiosities, *1925*

## EXCESS VERBIAGE

I savagely correct reports and drafts with a blue pencil. I cut them to ribbons, blot out the repetitions, mixed metaphors, circumlocutions, misspelled words and dreary Madison Avenue or technical clichés, and the same writers, perhaps a bit angry or chagrined, triumphantly send back the same tripe the next day. Either they are figuratively thumbing their noses at an idiosyncracy of the boss, or they are unteachable.

*Robert Moses, former New York Secretary of State, New York City parks commissioner, CEO, New York City Tunnel Authority and other municipal offices, on the need for clear and concise memos from his staff*

## EXCLUSIVITY

Members and Non-Members Only.

*Sign outside Mexico's Mandinga Disco in the Hotel Emporio, as reported in* Far Eastern Economic Review

## EXISTENTIALISM

I can't think of any new existing law that's in force that wasn't before.

*President George Bush, discussing import laws*

## EXPLANATIONS

. . . the story is the unveiling of the possibility of the impossibility of the unveiling.

*Professor H Hillis Miller, of the University of California at Irvine, about Nathaniel Hawthorne's short story 'The Minister's Black Veil', in his presentation, 'From the Theory of Reading to the Example Read'*

## EXPORTS

[The exports include] thumbscrews and cattle prods, just routine items for the police.

*Commerce Department spokesman on a regulation allowing the export of various products abroad*

## EXPOSING ONESELF

Nixon has been sitting in the White House while George McGovern has been exposing himself to the people of the United States.

*Frank Licht, then governor of Rhode Island, over vigorously campaigning for McGovern in the 1972 election*

What he does on his own time is up to him.

*Harlon Copeland, Sheriff of Bexar County, Texas, when one of his deputies was caught exposing himself to a child*

## Facts

Facts are stupid things.

*Ronald Reagan, misquoting John Adams in a speech to the Republican convention*

The single, overwhelming two facts were . . .

*Paddy Ashdown*

I'll tell you one fact – it may be rather boring but it's interesting.

*Barbara Cartland*

Some of the facts are true, some are distorted, and some are untrue.

*A State Department spokesman, commenting on an article in Foreign Policy*

Don't confuse me with the facts. I've got a closed mind.

*Earl Landgrebe, Republican congressman from Indiana and Nixon supporter, when told about incriminating conversations on the Watergate tapes*

The power of the head of state is not unlimited. Why is it said the power of the President is not unlimited? Probably the idea comes from the English translation: 'Is not unlimited.'

*Speaker of the Indonesian Parliament, Kharis Suhud, in a 1988 TV interview, quoted in the* Far Eastern Economic Review

## Facts of Life

Everyone who is for abortion was at one time a faeces.

*Peter Grace in an introduction to a Ronald Reagan speech; quoted on National Public Radio*

## Failure

Even Napoleon had his Watergate.

*Danny Ozark, Philadelphia Phillies manager, commenting about a Phillies' ten-game losing streak*

## Fame

When I write about anything the public makes a point to know nothing about it.

*Oliver Goldsmith, eighteenth-century Anglo-Irish poet, novelist and dramatist*

## Families

Music, sex and family are my greatest pleasures. Sex and family are the same thing to me.

*Simon Le Bon*

What really causes marital abuse is small families. If all women had a lot of brothers, this would never take place.

*Charles Poncy, Iowa State Representative (D-Ottumwa)*

The first would be our family. Your family, my family – which is composed of an immediate family of a wife and three children, a larger family with grandparents and aunts and uncles. We all have our family, whichever that may be.

*Dan Quayle, then vice-presidential candidate, during the 1988 campaign in a speech to Virginia schoolchildren*

## Famous Addresses

I've just returned from 10 Drowning Street, so I know what I'm talking about.

*Movie mogul, a Samuel Goldwyn in a political argument*

## Fashion

The cows started to look tired, something from last season. Buffalo are much more *sympathique*.

*Fashion designer, Yves Saint Laurent, on why he bought a herd of buffalo for his estate in Normandy*

## Feet

The clay feet of Germany will be revealed when we take off the gloves.

*Letter in the* Sunday Chronicle, *just before World War I*

Films

Once they were men. Now they are land crabs.

*Dialogue from* Attack of the Crab Monsters

Who ever heard of Casablanca? . . . I don't want to star opposite an unknown Swedish broad.

*George Raft, on the role of Rick in* Casablanca *(although some say he actually wanted the role and was merely expressing sour grapes)*

## Fire Extinguishers

I move, Mr Chairman, that all fire extinguishers be examined ten days before every fire.

*City councilman during debate*

## Firm Stands

[I am] pro-choice with limitations, pro-life with exceptions.

*Senator John Warner of Virginia, in a statement kicking off his bid for re-election*

## Fish

The Right Honourable Gentleman has gone to the top of the tree and caught a very big fish.

*Sir W Hart Dyke, MP*

## Fitness

If you're looking for a role model, you can't have someone who is not physically fit. Margaret Mead was a good role model, but she may not have looked good in a swimsuit.

*Leonard Horne, Miss America Pageant Director, on why a swimsuit competition is necessary*

## Flags

The new Irish flag would be orange and green, and would in future be known as the Irish tricolour.

*Smith O'Brien, Irish revolutionary*

## Flexibility

I've lived under situations where every decent man declared war first and I've lived under situations where you don't declare war. We've been flexible enough to kill people without declaring war.

*Lewis B Hershey, Lieutenant General and Director of the Selective Service System, on the Vietnam War*

## Flight Attendants

The stewardesses of Southwest Airlines must go through four steps, such as hardship, tiredment, dirt feeling. Beside the quality of general stewardess.

*From the first edition of Chinese airline Southwest Civil Aviation's* Inflight Magazing *(sic)*

## Food Subsidies

On the basis that it is essential and economical, economical for the country and for the Congress to have food available around here.

*Representative Jamie L Whitten (D-Miss) on why food subsidies were being cut for the poor – but kept for the House and Senate restaurants*

## Footwear

I have no weakness for shoes. I wear very simple shoes which are pump shoes. It is not one of my weaknesses.

*Imelda Marcos, former First Lady of the Philippines, and owner of 3,400 pairs of shoes*

## Fractions

The poor man was absolutely robbed by that accursed system by fully one-tenth of his hard earnings. Nay! he was sometimes deprived of as much as one-twentieth.

*Major O'Gorman, MP, discussing the Tithe Bill*

## Fraternal Organizations

Tolstoy was an unconscious Kiwanian.

*Edward Scheve in a speech to the Huntington Park, California, Kiwanis Club, as quoted in the* Watts Review

## Free Speech

When I want your opinion, I'll give it to you.

*Movie mogul, Samuel Goldwyn, to a young writer*

## Freedom



Man has been given his freedom to a greater extent than ever and that's quite wrong.

*Martha Mitchell, wife of former Attorney General John Mitchell*

Freedom of speech of the individual citizen must be based on the four basic principles of insisting on the socialist road, the dictatorship of the proletariat, the leadership of the party, and Marxism-Leninism-Mao Zedong thought. The citizen has only the freedom to support these principles and not the freedom to oppose them . . .

*People's Republic of China prosecutor, during the Wei Jingsheng case in 1979, in which defendant Wei, a human rights champion, cited the Chinese constitution guaranteeing free speech in his defence. He lost.*

## Freudian Slips

We need laws that protect everyone. Men and women, straights and gays, regardless of sexual perversion . . . ah, persuasion.

*Bella Abzug, New York politician, addressing a rally for the Equal Rights Amendment*

I am speaking of a great man who should have been President and would have been one of the greatest Presidents in history – Hubert Horatio Hornblower.

*Jimmy Carter in a speech at the 1980 democratic Convention*

For seven and a half years, I've worked alongside President Reagan. We've had triumphs. Made some mistakes. We've had some sex . . . uh . . . setbacks.

*George Bush*

The United States has much to offer the third world war.

*Ronald Reagan in a speech, on what the United States had to offer the Third World. He repeated this error nine times in the same speech*

## FRIENDSHIP

His friends are legendary. And I trusted him explicitly.

*Boxing announcer, Harry Balogh, on a famous boxing commissioner*

## FULFILMENT

My men grumble that they are frustrated – that there are no good targets left any more. But I always remind them of the plight of the pilots back in the States. 'Let's fact it,' I always tell them, 'Vietnam is the only place in the world today where you can drop real bombs.'

*A US Air Force wing commander during the Vietnam War*

## FUN

We have to pursue this subject of fun very seriously if we want to stay competitive in the twenty-first century.

*Singapore Minister of State for Finance and World Affairs, George Yeo*

## FUTURE

If we maintain our faith in God, our love of freedom and superior global air power, I think we can look to the future with confidence.

*General Curtis LeMay, in a speech given at Notre Dame's Washington's Birthday exercises, February 1956*

I believe we are on an irreversible trend towards more freedom and democracy. But that could change.

*Vice-President Dan Quayle*

We see nothing but increasingly brighter clouds every month.

*President Gerald Ford, on the economy, to a group of Michigan businessmen*

We are not ready for any unforeseen event that may or may not occur.

*Vice-President Dan Quayle in an interview with the* Cleveland Plain Dealer

We should not look at the immediate situation in terms of planning a new move in any time-frame that is now immediately foreseeable.

*Henry Kissinger, Secretary of State, speaking to the Senate Foreign Relations Committee*

It's a question of whether we're going to go forward into the future, or past to the back.

*Vice-President Dan Quayle*

## Yogi Berra

Lorenzo Pietro Berra, or Lawrence Peter Berra, better known as Yogi Berra, is an American institution.

A great New York Yankee catcher and manager of both the New York Yankees and Mets, elected three times as the American League's most valuable player, Berra was noted on field for his hitting and catching, and off field for his pithy way of saying the wrong thing in a way that made the Yogi-ism wiser and more meaningful than the right way of saying it. For example, there's a lot of wisdom in Yogi's.

You got to be careful if you don't know where you're going, because you might not get there.

Of course, other Yogi-isms are just plain fun. When someone asked Manager Yogi if Don Mattingly's performance as a first baseman had exceeded his expectations, Yogi answered: 'I'd say he's done more than that.'

Many Yogi-isms may have been attributed to Yogi rather than actually said by him. And some things he said evolved a bit in the re-telling. For example, a careful *Sports Illustrated* survey found that Yogi's famous 'It ain't over till it's over' probably began as 'You're not out of it till you're out of it' and so on until it became the quintessential Yogi-ism in its final, pithy form.

But no matter. The fun of Yogi-isms is the fun of them, whether he actually said them or not. And he himself admitted he often didn't remember if he said a specific Yogi-ism or not. So, when reading Yogi, remember what Yogi said:

I could've probably said that.

*Some of Yogi's best:*

I want to thank all these who made this night necessary. (Addressing the crowd at a 1947 event in his honour)

You give a hundred per cent in the first half of the game, and if it isn't enough, in the second half you give what's left.

How can you say this and that when this and that hasn't happened yet?

If you can't imitate him, don't copy him.

A nickel ain't worth a dime any more.

I don't know, I'm not in shape yet. (When asked his cap size)

He is a big clog in their machine. (Reportedly talking about Ted Williams)

I got a touch of pantomime poisoning. (Explaining to his manager, Casey Stengel, why he couldn't play a game)

If I didn't wake up, I'd still be sleeping.

How can you think and hit at the same time?

I wish I had an answer to that because I'm getting tired of answering that question. (In response to a question about the 1984 Yankees' dismal record)

## Gay Rights

It's easier to thump a faggot than an average Joe. Who cares?

*A Los Angeles police officer, quoted in the* Christopher Commission Report

## Geography

You mean there are two Koreas?

*A US Ambassador-designate to the Far East, after being asked his opinion during congressional hearings on the North Korea–South Korea conflict, as reported by government officials*

Ballarat is the fairest city south of the hemisphere.

*Edward Murphy, Legislative Assemblyman from Victoria, Australia*

The town of Albany contains 500 dwelling houses and 2,400 inhabitants, all standing with their gable ends to the street.

*Morse's Geography, the premier geography textbook in the United States during the 1800s*

I favour this irrigation bill in order that we may turn the barren hills of my state into fruitful valleys.

*A senator, as reported by Massachusetts State Senator, John F Parker, in support of a port-barrel bill*

This is morally repugnant to millions of people, not only in the United States, but also in the 24th Congressional District.

*Representative Alfred Santangelo of New York, in a debate on setting up a national lottery*

## GEORGIA

Georgia produces enough fine apples each year for every man, woman and child in the state to have two bushels.

Georgia's sanitarium for the insane has for the past year every bed occupied and many waiting to be taken in.

*From the* Atlanta Constitution, *1924*

## GETTING AHEAD

It's not politics, it's just who you know.

*Paul Guanzon, sportscaster, on how to become one*

It's about 90 per cent strength and 40 per cent technique.

*Johnny Walker, world middleweight wrist-wrestling champion, on what it takes to be a champ*

## Getting along with Others

Contrary to popular belief, I have always had a wonderful repertoire with my players.

*Danny Ozark, Philadelphia Phillies manager*

## Gift of the Gab

Well, I think that's a – it's had some difficult times but I think we have – we, I think, have been able to make some very good progress and it's – I would say that it's – it's – it's delightful that we're able to – to share the time and the relationship that we – that we do share.

*Senator Edward Kennedy, during a 4 November 1979 on-air interview with Roger Mudd, trying to answer the question, 'What is the present state of your marriage?'*

Well, I'm going to kick that one right into the end zone of the Secretary of Education. But, yes, we have all – he travels a good deal, goes abroad. We have a lot of people in the department that does that. We're having an international – this is not as much education as dealing with the environment – a big international conference coming up. And we get it all the time – exchange of ideas.

*President George Bush, in February 1990, answering a high-school student's questions about whether the Bush administration was getting ideas on education from other countries.*

But let me – I better switch over here for some more – and may I – a question – and I don't mean to offend with regard to follow-up – and I understand why you had them, but we've been reduced to the number of questions we get to ask when everybody has a follow-up. So ask them both at once.

*President Ronald Reagan during a 1984 press conference*

## GLOVES

I'm wearing these gloves for my hands.

*Yogi Berra, when asked why he was wearing gloves*

## GOD

I can't understand how all this can happen. It's enough to make one lose one's faith in God!

*Eva Braun, writing to a friend from Hitler's bunker during the siege and bombing of Berlin in April 1945*

I believe that, next to God, Andrew Jackson was the greatest man who ever lived.

*John Trotwood Moore, State Historian of Tennessee, 1920s*

## GOLD CLUBS

[A gun is] a recreational tool, like a golf club or a tennis racket. You can kill someone with a golf club, you know.

*Martel Lovelace, NRA official*

## Good Advice

Light pranks add zest to your services, but don't pull the customers' ears.

*From the Japanese Tourist Industry Board, Rules for Hotel Chambermaids, 1936*

You are invited to take advantage of the chambermaid.

*From a guest directory at a Japanese hotel, 1991*

## Good News

The good news is the war is over. The bad news is we lost.

*White House photographer David Hume Kennerly, running into the Oval Office on the day Saigon fell to the Communists*

## Good Taste

We'll have a recording broadcast a fire fight, mortars exploding, bullets flying, Vietnamese screaming . . . There's nothing offensive about it.

*A spokesperson for Vietnam Village, a 1976 Florida tourist theme park that reproduced a Vietnamese village during the war, complete with 56 Vietnamese refugees playing the parts of the villagers, describing what will happen after a tour group enters the park*

## GOVERNMENT

You know we have three great branches of this government of ours. . . . We have a strong President, supposedly in the White House. We have a strong Congress, supposedly in the legislative branch. We have a strong Supreme Court, supposedly heading the judiciary system.

*President Gerald Ford in a 1974 speech*

I am the Secretary for Trade and Industry.

*Social Security Secretary, Peter Lilley, introducing himself to a committee*

No unmet needs exist and . . . current unmet needs that are being met will continue to be met.

*Transportation Commission on Unmet Transit Needs, Mariposa County, California*

## GRAMMAR

Tenses, Gender and Number. For the purpose of the rules and regulations contained in this chapter, the present tense includes the past and future tenses, and the future, the present; the masculine gender includes the feminine, and the feminine, the masculine, and the singular includes the plural, and the plural the singular.

*In the revised (1973) state code for the Department of Consumer Affairs, California*

## Graves

. . . the empty grave where all our ruined industries lie.

*J Ramsay MacDonald, then leader of the Labour Party in the House of Commons, later Prime Minister, during a parliamentary debate*

## Great Expectations

As the Reagan presidency ends, it is time for the Bush pregnancy to begin.

*Tommy Thompson, Wisconsin governor, anticipating Bush's inauguration*

## Greeks

Retraction: The Greek Special is a huge 18-inch pizza and not a huge 18-inch penis, as . . . described in [an ad]. Blondie's Pizza would like to apologize for any confusion Friday's ad might have caused.

*A correction printed in the* Daily Californian, *cited in Ronald D Pasquariello's 1990* Almanac of Quotable Quotes

## Green Berets

In a way, we're a kind of Peace Corps.

*Training director of the Fort Bragg Green Beret Center in 1969*

## Growth

Sustainable growth is growth that is sustainable.

*John Major*

## Guilty, or not

[Hijackers should be given] a rapid trial . . . with due process of law at the airport, then hanged.

*Edward Davis, police chief of Los Angeles in 1973*

## Gymnastics

The pale face of the British soldier is the backbone of our Indian Army.

*Scottish MP in debate*

They would never agree to peace so long as Prussian militarism held its head above water to trample underfoot our liberties.

*Sir Edward Carson, Anglo-Irish politician (and lawyer who cross-examined Oscar Wilde), talking about World War I*

She disentangled her foot in the netting and wound it up.

*George Eliot, English novelist, writing in a novel*

Gentlemen, a member of this House had taken advantage of my absence to tweak my nose behind my back. I hope that the next time he abuses me behind my back like a coward he will do it to my face like a man, and not go skulking into the thicket to assail a gentleman who isn't present to defend himself.

*An MP from Ballarat East, Australia*

Against every bone in my body, I'm sitting here twisting both arms.

*Representative Claude De Bruhl, North Carolina state legislator, when voting for a bill he opposed*

They pushed their nomination down my throat behind my back.

*J Ramsay MacDonald, then MP, later the first Labour Prime Minister in the 1920s and 30s, modestly denying any role in the honour he was about to receive*

## Hairs, Splitting of

We didn't turn him down. We didn't accept him.

*Springdale Golf Club (Princeton, NJ) president explaining why a black applicant was rejected*

## Hawaii

Hawaii has always been a very pivotal role in the Pacific. It is in the Pacific. It is a part of the United States that is an island that is right here.

*Vice-President Dan Quayle, during a visit to Hawaii in 1989*

## Health

I've been laid up with the intentional flu.

*Movie mogul, Samuel Goldwyn*

## Hearing

So long as Ireland remains silent on this question England will be deaf to our entreaties.

*Irish politician, late 1880s*

HELPFUL HINTS

WARNING: Never use while sleeping.

*Warnings with hair dryer, cited in* US News & World Report

REPLACING BATTERY: Replace the old battery with a new one.

*Directions for a mosquito repellent, reported in* Far Eastern Economic Review

## HISTORY

We have to go back centuries for a parallel to such treatment, and even then we don't find it.

*Anonymous speaker during a Parliamentary debate*

## HOLIDAYS

Today is Father's Day, so everyone out there: Happy Birthday!

*Ralph Kiner, announcer for the New York Mets*

## HONESTY

He's trying to take the decision out of the hands of twelve honest men and give it to 435 Congressmen!

*Representative Charles Vanik of Ohio, when he heard that the indicted Spiro Agnew was asking to have his corruption case tried by the House instead of in a regular court*

## Horses

Bring on the empty horses!

*Director Michael Curtiz, telling film crew to bring on (riderless) horses for filming*

## House of Representatives

Republican Dan Rostenkowski (acting as Chairman): Title IX of the recorded bill is now title X.

Republican William L Dickinson: So there is no title IX. There is title XX and we have re-opened title VIII, if I am correct.

Rostenkowski: A new title IX was inserted by amendment, so there is now a title IX and a title X.

Dickinson: There is a title VIII, there is a title IX, there is a title X, is that correct?

Rostenkowski: Title X is the last title in the bill.

Dickinson: So an amendment to either title VIII or title IX or title X would be in order at this time?

Rostenkowski: Not title IX. Just title VIII and title X are open to amendment.

Dickinson: Well, I had an amendment that I would like to offer. I thought it was to title IX if there is a title IX.

Rostenkowski: If the gentleman's amendment was drafted to title IX, it will be in order to title X.

DICKINSON: Mr Chairman, I have an amendment at the desk which I would like to offer to title VIII.

*A few moments of discussion on the floor of the House of Representatives in 1982, as reported by* The Washington Monthly

## HUMAN KIDNEYS

No one as yet had exhibited the structure of human kidneys, Vesalius having only examined them in dogs.

*Henry Hallam, famous Oxford historian, in his monumental work,* A View of the State of Europe in the Middle Ages, *1818*

## HUMAN RIGHTS

The rights you have are the rights given to you by Committee. We will determine what rights you have and what rights you have not got.

*J Parnell Thomas, House Un-American Affairs Committee, to a witness*

You hear about constitutional rights, free speech and the free press. Every time I hear these words I say to myself, 'That man is a Red, that man is a Communist!' You never hear a real American talk like that.

*Mayor Frank Hague, Jersey City, New Jersey, 1938*

## HUNGER

There shouldn't be hunger, at least hunger unnecessarily of the people who would want otherwise to be fed.

*Robert Carleson, Office of Policy Development*

## HUNGER-STRIKER

He's bitten off a bit more than he can chew.

*Brother of Hunger-striker Raymond McCreesh*

## HUSTON, JOHN

John, if you weren't the son of my beloved friend, Walter Huston, and if you weren't a brilliant writer, a fine actor and a magnificent director – you'd be nothing but a common drunk.

*Gregory Ratoff, producer, to John Huston, after John Huston refused to make a film history of his life*

## Ideas

I had a great idea this morning, but I didn't like it.

*Movie mogul, Samuel Goldwyn*

## Identities, Mistaken

Due to a typing error, Governor Dukakis was incorrectly identified in the third paragraph as Mike Tyson.

Fitchburg-Leominster Sentinel and Enterprise *correction*

## Immigrants

When I go to hotels in mid-town for various conventions and awards ceremonies, I am continually served my food and drink by someone who not only isn't black, but can't even speak English. These people take home all excess food, including soda and in some cases wine.

*Hazel Dukes, civil rights activist and New York City Off-Track Betting Corporation chief*

## IMMUTABILITY

This strategy represents our policy for all time. Until it's changed.

*Marlin Fitzwater, White House spokesperson under George Bush, on a just-released national security strategy*

## INCEST

Inbreeding is how we get championship horses.

*Carl Gunter, Louisiana state representative, explaining why he was fighting a proposed anti-abortion bill that allowed abortion in cases of incest*

## INDIA

India is the finest climate under the sun; but a lot of young fellows come out here, and they drink and they eat, and they drink and they die: and then they write home to their parents a pack of lies, and say it's the climate that has killed them.

*Sir Colin Campbell, British officier charged by British War Department to report on morale problems with the British Army in India*

## INFORMATION

Information is voluntary. Failure to provide information could subject individual to be called on extended active duty when member might be eligible for assignment to Standby Reserve . . .

*Privacy Act Statement, US Air Force Reserve, mid-70s*

## Injuries

Benedict may not be hurt as much as he really is.

*Jerry Coleman, announcer for the San Diego Padres, talking about a player's injury during on-air game coverage*

The doctors X-rayed my head and found nothing.

*Baseball greaty Dizzy Dean explaining how he felt after being hit on the head by a ball in the 1934 World Series*

## Innovation

We're launching this innovation for the first time.

*New York City Mayor, Jimmy Walker*

## Instruction, Easy to Follow

I'm the football coach around here and don't you remember it.

*Ex-Houston Oiler and Florida State coach, Bill Petersen*

Fans, don't fail to miss tomorrow's game.

*Dizzy Dean*

## Integrity

Grassley praised Senate colleagues 'for making tough decisions to close tax loopholes which have led to abuses', and said he was particularly pleased at the Senate's willingness to protect farmers through a special concession.

*In a press release from the office of Senator Charles E Grassley, Iowa Republican, quoted in* The Washington Monthly

## INTEGRITY

I suppose I felt my votes on these issues would carry me on the integrity image on all these other things I got careless on. I have come to the conclusion I have let my integrity become restricted to the issues too much, and not enough, perhaps, to every act and procedure of my office.

*Oregon Senator Mark Hatfield, in a* Portland Oregonian *article, commenting on the gifts and free tuition for his son he was given by James Holderman, the (indicted) president for the University of South Carolina.*

## INTELLIGENCE

The infiltration group was composed of one third males, one third females and one third party officials.

*From a military intelligence document during the Vietnam War*

This unit had an estimated strength of about 2,000 men, of which 300 were women.

*From a military intelligence document during the Vietnam War*

## INTERRUPTIONS

Don't talk to me while I'm interrupting.

*Director, Michael Curtiz*

Keep quiet, you're always interrupting me in the middle of my mistakes.

*Director, Michael Curtiz*

## Inventing

It is curious to observe the various substitutes for paper before its invention.

*Isaac D'Israeli, noted author and father of British Prime Minister Benjamin Disraeli, in his book,* Curiosities of Literature

## Invisibility

Unseen powers, like the deities of Homer in the war of Troy, were seen to mingle at every step with the tide of sublimary affairs.

*Sir Archibald Alison, famous nineteenth-century Scottish historian and lawyer, author of multi-volume histories of France, in his review of Guizot*

## Irrevocability

I am giving you a chance to redeem your character, something you have irretrievably lost.

*Serjeant Arabin, famous London justice, Advocate General in the Whig government of the late 1830s*

## Jail-Building

1. Resolved, by this council, that we build a new jail.
2. Resolved, that the new jail be built out of the materials of the old jail.
3. Resolved, that the old jail be used until the new jail is finished.

*resolution of Board of Councilmen, Canton, Mississippi, mid-1800s*

## Judgment

There's no textbook on judgment. I might make one or two other (mistakes), but it will certainly be with great forethought.

*Marion Barry, Mayor of Washington DC*

## Jumping the Gun

I am in control here. As of now, I am in control here in the White House

*Alexander Haig, then Secretary of State, after President Reagan was shot, forgetting that in actuality he was fourth in line of succession*

If a person is innocent of a crime, then he is not a suspect.

*Then-Attorney General Edwin Meese explaining to the American Bar Association why the Miranda decision enabling those arrested to be advised of their rights was not necessary anymore*

## Keeping Quiet at Meetings

A little less quiet please, Mr Blackbird.

*New York Athletic Commissioner General John J Phelan, to boxer Joe Louis's trainer, 'Chappie' Blackburn*

## Kiddie Shows

I want you to take your balls in your hands and bounce them on the floor and then throw them as high as you can. Now, have you all got your balls in your hands?

*Announcer of children's radio show,* Life with Mother, *to her little audience, as reported by Geoffrey Moorhouse*

## Killing

WISH: to end all the killing in the world

HOBBIES: hunting and fishing

*From personal statistics of California Angel Bryan Harvey, flashed on the scoreboard at Anaheim Stadium, 1989*

## Knee Surgery

I've never had major knee surgery on any other part of my body.

*Winston Bennett, University of Kentucky basketball forward*

## Knowledge

The President is aware of what is going on. That's not to say there is something going on.

*Ron Ziegler, press secretary to President Richard Nixon, on a rumour that allied forces were attacking the Laotian border*

## Ladies

(The commotion) has something to do with a fat lady.

*Dizzy Dean, baseball great turned sports announcer, explaining why there was a hubbub in the stands during a St Louis Browns game he was covering*

I've just been informed that the fat lady is the Queen of Holland.

*Dizzy Dean, on air a few minutes later, after a studio executive quietly told him that the 'fat lady' was actually the Queen of the Netherlands*

## Language

I'm no linguist, but I have been told that in the Russian language there isn't even a word for freedom.

*President Ronald Reagan on why Russia was still – and presumably always would be – communist, overlooking the word* svoboda, *or freedom*

Every monumental inscription should be in Latin; for that being a dead language it will ever live.

*Samuel Johnson, eighteenth-century English writer, in a blunder noted by his contemporaries*

## Law

There has been much talk here this afternoon about the law of the land. We are makers of the law of the land and makers of the law of the land ought to understand and respect the law of the land.

*Senator Roger W Jepsen, Republican from Iowa, during a congressional debate*

## Leader

Let the first contingent go ahead and I will send a man after you to lead the way.

*J C Percy, bicycle club leader, addressing the group*

## Leadership

Well, it's um, you know, you have to come to grips with the different issues that, ah . . . we're facing, I mean we have . . . we have to deal with each of the various questions that we're talking about whether it's a question of the economy, whether it's in the area of energy.

*Senator Edward Kennedy, during his 4 November 1979 on-air interview with Roger Mudd, explaining why he would be different than then President Jimmy Carter*

## Legal Defences

Did you get a good look at my face when I took your purse?

*Accused thief who undertook his own defence at his trial, to his alleged victim, as reported in the* National Review. *He got ten years*

## Legal Definitions

Buttocks: The area at the rear of the human body (sometimes referred to as the glutaeus maximus) which lies between two imaginary lines running parallel to the ground when a person is standing, the first or top of such line being one-half inch below the top of the vertical cleavage of the nates (i.e., the back of the leg) and the second or bottom line being one-half inch above the lowest point of curvature of the fleshy protuberance (sometimes referred to as the gluteal fold), and between two imaginary lines, one on each side of the body (the 'outside lines'), which outside lines are perpendicular to the ground and to the horizontal lines described above and which perpendicular outside lines pass through the outermost point(s) at which each nate meets the outer side of each leg . . .

*Part of a St Augustine, Florida, ordinance drafted by city commissioners to regulate nudity on the beach and in restaurants*

## Legal Ordinances

Section 4: Licenses shall be issued only to persons of good moral turpitude.

*Clearwater, Florida, city ordinance on liquor licences*

## LETTING IT ALL (ALMOST) HANG OUT

PRESIDENT RICHARD NIXON: Do you think we want to go this route now? Let it all hang out, so to speak?

JOHN DEAN: Well, it isn't really that.

H R HALDEMAN: It's a limited hang-out.

JOHN EHRLICHMAN: It's a modified, limited hang out.

## LIES

If I tell a lie it's only because I think I'm telling the truth.

*Phil Gaglardi, Minister of Highways in British Columbia, Canada*

I was not lying, I said things that later on seemed to be untrue.

*Richard Nixon, discussing Watergate on a 1978 interview*

Thus, the black lie, issuing from his base throat, becomes a boomerang to his hand, and he is hoist by his own petard, and finds himself a marked man.

*Newspaper editor in Wisconsin*

## LIFE

It's not a matter of life and death. It's more important than that.

*Lou Duva, on the upcoming fight of his protege against boxer Mike Tyson*

## On Life After Death

If Lincoln were alive today, he'd roll over in his grave.

*President Gerald Ford*

Yogi Berra (during a 20 Questions game): Is he living?

Teammate: Yes

Yogi: Is he living now?

If Cal Coolidge were alive today to witness this scene, he'd roll over in his grave.

*Representative in Massachussetts House*

## Life and Death

Smoking kills. If you're killed, you've lost a very important part of your life.

*Brooke Shields, said to demonstrate why she should become spokesperson for a federal anti-smoking campaign*

## Life Insurance

I'll get it when I die.

*Yogi Berra, explaining why he bought a life insurance policy*

## Light and Darkness

The light which the Lord Chancellor had thrown upon the matter was darkness.

*Lord Ribblesdale, British aristocrat and Master of the Buckhounds in the 1890s called 'the Ancestor' because of his patrician good looks*

## ABRAHAM LINCOLN

It is indeed fitting that we gather here today to pay tribute to Abraham Lincoln, who was born in a log cabin that he built with his own hands.

*an unnamed politician in a speech honouring Lincoln, as reported by Senator Morris K ('Mo') Udall*

## LINKAGES

I love California. I grew up in Phoenix.

*Vice President Dan Quayle*

## LOGIC

I desire what is good. Therefore, everyone who does not agree with me is a traitor.

*George III*

## LONGEVITY

A lot of people my age are dead at the present time.

*Casey Stengel, baseball great, Yankees and Mets manager*

## LOVE SCENES

Could you get a little closer apart?

*Michael Curtiz, Hollywood director, to two stars*

## LYING

(It is) not fair to say that I have misinformed Congress of other Cabinet officers. I haven't testified to that.

I've testified that I withheld information from Congress. And with regard to the Cabinet officers, I didn't withhold anything from them that they didn't want withheld from them.

*Rear Admiral John Poindexter, in his testimony to a congressional hearing looking into the Iran-Contra affair*

The President misspoke himself.

*Attributed to Ron Ziegler, Nixon's press secretary*

I apologize for lying to you... I promise I won't deceive you except in matters of this sort.

*Spiro T Agnew, Vice-President under Nixon, speaking to reporters about his assertions that he wouldn't be going to Cambodia. He made this apology on the plane headed to Phnom Penh, Cambodia*

## Machismo and Pestilence

In the early sixties we were strong, we were virulent.

*John Connally, Secretary of Treasury under Richard Nixon, in an early 70s' speech, as reported in a contemporary* American Scholar

## Man in Space

The United States is at peace with all the world, and sustains friendly relations with the rest of mankind.

*President Benjamin Harrison in a speech to Congress*

## Manure

. . . when floors are wet and slippery with manure, you can have a bad fall.

*From the US Occupational Safety and Health Administration's booklet,* Safety with Beef Cattle *1976*

## Mardi Gras

Even if they had it in the streets, I wouldn't go.

*Attributed to movie mogul Samuel Goldwyn*

## Mayors

I am not the leader of Washington. I am not the business leader of Washington. I am not the spiritual leader of Washington. I am not the civic leader of Washington. I am not the social leader of Washington. I am the political leader of Washington. That's where my responsibility ends.

*Marion Barry, Mayor of Washington DC, defending himself against critics who held his lack of leadership partly responsible for the high murder rate in DC.*

## Meat Eating

In the whole history of the world, whenever a meat-eating race has gone to war against a non-meat eating race, the meat-eaters won. It produces superior people. We have the books of history.

*Senator Carl Curtis (R-Neb.) during a debate on banning DES as a food additive for livestock, 1975*

## Mediocrity

Even if he were mediocre, there are a lot of mediocre judges and people and lawyers. Don't they deserve some representation on the court?

*Senator Roman Hruska (R-Neb.), defending Judge Harold Carswell, the first Nixon nominee for the Supreme Court, against charges that he was mediocre*

## Mental Illness

My boyfriend is a split personality – a kind of Jekyll of all trades.

*Dorothy Stickney's (theatre and film actress from the thirties through the fifties) manicurist*

## Metaphors

Since the government has let the cat out of the bag there is nothing to do but take the bull by the horns.

*Jeremiah MacVeagh, MP*

When shall the lion of autocracy walk hand in hand with the floodgates of democracy?

*James Sexton, MP, in a speech*

The apple of discord is now fairly in our midst, and if not nipped in the bud, it will burst forth in a conflagration which will deluge society in an earthquake of bloody apprehension.

*Nebraska newspaper editorial, circa 1870, reporting on legislative turmoil*

The gutless, no-good 100th Congress . . . will write off freedom in Nicaragua, throw them to the alligators, and hope the alligators will eat someone else and eat us last and they can peel off a slice of that salami and they will not bother us for now. Do not rock the boat.

*Senator Steve Symms (R-Idaho)*

It is no use for the honourable member to shake his head in the teeth of his own words.

*William E Gladstone, leader of the Liberal Party of England and Prime Minister, in a speech*

As we debate this bill, that sword of Damocles is hanging over Pandora's box.

*From New York City Council debates, quoted by Molly Ivins,* New York Times Magazine

[This item is] a mere fleabite in the ocean of our expenditure.

*Lord Randolph Churchill, father of Winston, during a Parliament debate*

## Method Acting

. . . the greatest villain that ever lived, a man worse than Hitler or Stalin. I am speaking of Sigmund Freud.

*Telly Savalas, actor, discussing a role he was going to play*

## Middle-east Crisis

Why can't the Jews and the Arabs just sit down together and settle this like good Christians?

*Overheard during a congressional debate; also attributed to Arthur Balfour, British statesman, Prime Minister and Foreign Secretary*

## Mid-Term

As a compensating measure, the focus of shorter- and longer-term analyses would be extended to include the mid-term. Although this approach will in some measure reduce the comprehensive nature of the intended analysis, the compromise will provide adequate data for meaningful progress toward integrative policy development.

*Department of Energy's revolutionary decision to include all the stuff in the middle, from the 1981* Budget Revision Report

## Military Intelligence

It is necessary for technical reasons that these warheads should be stored with the top at the bottom, and the bottom at the top. In order that there may be no doubt as to which is the top and which is the bottom, for storage purposes, it will be seen that the bottom of each head has been labelled with the word TOP.

*British Admiralty instruction dealing with the storage of warheads and torpedoes (quoted in* Outrageous Quotations*)*

## Military Preparedness

We have permitted our naval capability to deteriorate. At the same time we are better than we were a few years ago.

*Caspar Weinberger, Secretary of Defense, on the ups and downs of the US Navy in 1982*

## Military Spending

I think there are very few indeed who try to take advantage of their former positions in the military to sell us defence products . . . Most officers are not salesmen. A friend of mine who retired told me, 'The idea of going back and trying to peddle products on the basis of my military friendships is so repulsive that I would rather starve to death.'

*US Army General Earle Wheeler, former chairman of the joint Chiefs of Staff, 1969.*

## Minds

What a waste it is to lose one's mind – or not to have a mind. How true that is.

*Vice-President Dan Quayle addressing a United Negro College Fund affair and garbling their slogan – 'A mind is a terrible thing to waste'*

## Modern Art

Anyone who sees and paints a sky green and pastures blue ought to be sterilized.

*Adolf Hitler, painter of stiff, inhuman cityscapes and sponsor of the Aryan art movement which lost popularity after April 1945*

## Modernity

Let's bring it up to date with some snappy nineteenth-century dialogue.

*Movie mogul Samuel Goldwyn*

## Money

In the prosecution of the present war, every man ought to be ready to give his last guinea to protect the remainder.

*Chancellor of the Exchequer, Sir John Parnell, in the Irish House of Commons, 1795, during a debate on the leather tax*

## Money

The directors' fees have been hardly earned.

*Chairman of a brewery, trying (and failing) to defend his board of directors and a poor balance sheet*

## Money

I'd find the fellow who lost it, and if he was poor I'd return it.

*Yogi Berra, answering Casey Stengel's question, 'What would you do if you found a million dollars?'*

I'll fight him for nothing if the price is right.

*Marlon Starling, WBA welterweight, talking about fighting the titlest Lloyd Honeygham*

## Motherhood

That's what (golf) really needs – some striking female to take over and become the next superstar. It would have been Nancy Lopez, but Nancy turned to motherhood and so has her body.

*Frank Chirkinian, producer for CBS Sports*

## Mouth-Watering Names for Soft Drinks

Bite the wax tadpole.

*Coca-cola name as originally translated into Chinese. It was changed to mean 'May the mouth rejoice'*

## Movie Stars

He (Steve McQueen) must have made that before he died.

*Yogi Berra about a Steve McQueen film*

## Movies with Sound

Novelty is always welcome, but talking pictures are just a fad.

*Irving Thalberg, MGM production head in the late 1920s*

## Music

Among the interrelated matters of a time and place, Muzak is a thing that fits in.

*Chairman of the board of scientific advisers of Muzak, as quoted in Edwin Newman's* Strictly Speaking

Muzak promotes the sharing of meaning because it massifies symbolism in which not few, but all, can participate.

*Chairman of the board of scientific advisers of Muzak, as quoted in Edwin Newman's* Strictly Speaking

(The US Navy urgently) needs modern musicians.

*Michael Dukakis, 1988 Democratic presidential candidate, during a campaign speech. He meant munitions*

## Samuel Goldwyn

Samuel Goldwyn probably would have preferred to be remembered only as one of the founders of the Hollywood film industry. But Goldwyn's mangled syntax has entered our language and culture, and along with *The Best Years of Our Lives*, for which he won an Oscar, Sam Goldwyn is remembered for such convolutions as his immortal:

Any man who goes to a psychiatrist ought to have his head examined.

Goldwyn was born in Poland but came to the United States early in his life, in time to help found the Hollywood film industry. Along with Jesse Lasky and Cecil B De Mille, he organized the Jesse Lasky film company in 1916. Later he struck off on his own with the Goldwyn Production Company, which was then merged with Louis B Mayer's company to form Metro-Goldwyn-Mayer, probably the most powerful Hollywood studio. Describing his own career, Goldwyn supposedly said:

I was always an independent, even when I had partners.

And so he went on to produce independently such classics as *Wuthering Heights* and *Guys and Dolls*.

Along the way, he became famous for his 'Goldwyn-isms', which delighted the Hollywood community and, as with anything else in Hollywood that becomes successful, spawned hundreds of imitations. The question with a Goldwyn-ism, then, is did he actually say it or was it coined by some Hollywood flack or gossip columnist? Goldwyn himself towards the end of his life ended up denying he ever said many of his best – but by this time he was sick and tired of them.

Some are clearly false. 'I can answer you in two words – im possible' is an old joke and was (probably) not said by Goldwyn at all. On the other hand, the famous, 'Gentlemen, include me out' is most likely *bona fide*, and not apocryphal as long believed. But as with Yogi Berra and Sir Boyle Roche, it really doesn't matter whether he said it or not. Like Boyle Roche and Yogi Berra, Goldwyn deserves much credit for exploring new linguistic territory. As he (supposedly) said:

I've gone where the hand of man has never set foot.

Some of Goldwyn's best:

Give me a smart idiot over a stupid genius any day.

Why call him Joe? Every Tom, Dick and Harry is called Joe.

I want you to cohabit with me. (Asking a female writer to collaborate on a story with him)

You've got to take the bull by the teeth.

I read part of it all the way through.

I love the ground I walk on.

You write with great warmth and charmth. (apocryphal)

A verbal contract isn't worth the paper it's written on.

I ran into George Kaufman last night. He was at my house for dinner.

I'm going out for some tea and trumpets.

When asked by his secretary if she could destroy some old files: Go ahead. But make copies of them first.

When told a director was 'too caustic': To hell with cost, pay him what he wants.

## Names

Ah yes, Mohammed – that's one of the most common Christian names in the world.

*Kid Jensen*

## Napalm

Well, it seems pretty ridiculous to me that people can be so emotional about how you kill people. What's so bad about nape anyway?

*Pilot at Danang Air Force Base, 1970*

## Natural Disasters

It should have a big exciting finish – like an earthquake, a catechism of nature.

*Harry Rapf, high ranking MGM executive in the 30s and 40s*

## Nature

I happen to be one of those people who thinks the aesthetics of a place are improved by putting a nice transmission line through it.

*Montana Power Company Chairman Jo McElwain, quoted in the* Portland Oregonian

The wild animals love to traverse over packed-down snowmobile tracks, for these machines do just that, pack the snow and do no harm to the growth underneath. Snowmobiles actually make it possible for the animals to move through their habitat just a bit easier.

*Al Donohue, Chairman of the Montana Tourism Advisory Council,* Great Falls Tribune

It's unfair that it remains empty and unspoiled.

*Hugh Stone, developer of a proposed subdivision, on delays in permits to begin construction*

## Nature Lovers

I have a great feeling for the soil. My brother is the leading conservationalist in the world and I just love sitting on my bulldozer and experiencing nature.

*Golfer, Gary Player, quoted in the* Sarasota Herald-Tribune, *on his plans to build new golf courses in Florida*

## Nazism

Thorough mastication avoids needless waste and payment of unnecessary expenses to foreign countries.

*From the Storm Trooper paper,* Das Schwarze Korps

## Nixon Impersonators

There are guys that can talk like Nixon and sound like him, and I don't even believe the tapes are authentic.

*Earl F Landgrebe, former Indiana representative, discussing why it may not have been Nixon's voice on the Nixon tapes*

## Non sequiturs



Look, I want to give the high five symbol to high tech . . . the truth is, it reminds a lot of people of the way I pitch horseshoes. Would you believe some of the people? Would you believe our dog?

*George Bush in a speech given at a Ford Aerospace plant*

## Nuclear Attack

It would be a good thing to take your bankbook to the fallout shelter with you.

*Federal Reserve System suggestion*

## Nuclear Attack

During state of national emergency resulting from enemy attack, the essential functions of the Service will be as follows: (1) assessing, collecting, and recording taxes . . .

Internal Revenue Service Handbook *1976*

Actual meltdown takes three to five days, and that's enough time to evacuate Long Island

*George Koop, legislative candidate in Suffolk County, on New York's Long Island, in support of a local nuclear power plant*

## NUCLEAR POWER

Nuclear power is the cleanest, the most efficient, and the most economical energy source, with no environmental problems.

*President Ronald Reagan quoted in a 1980* Sierra *magazine, before various nuclear disasters in the 1980s*

## NUCLEAR WAR

QUESTION: Do you think there could be a battlefield exchange without having buttons pressed all the way up the line?

PRESIDENT REAGAN: Well, I would – if they realized that we – if we went back to that stalemate, only because our retaliatory power, our seconds, or our strike at them after their first strike would be so destructive that they couldn't afford it, that would hold them off.

Some programmes have been theatrical masterpieces, but all we're seeing is the negative side of nuclear war.

*Senator Barry Goldwater, discussing television shows about the nuclear war*

In fact, living standards within the first year following either attack (UNCLX or CIVLOG) could compare favourably with those enjoyed in this country in the late 1950s.

The net effect of the attack indicates a reduction in per capita value-added of approximately $660.

*Two economists speaking at a Fort Monroe, Virginia, seminar sponsored by Civil Defense in 1967. A UNCLX (300 megaton) attack would kill half the population of the United States*

It is also quite likely that the general public finds the thought of nuclear attack so horrible that the additional horror of a post-attack policy for wealth distribution would be considered of marginal importance.

*Henry Peskin, Office of Emergency Planning*

## Nuclear Weapons

This kind of weapon can't help but have an effect on the population as a whole.

*President Ronald Reagan*

Atomic energy might be as good as our present-day explosives, but it is unlikely to produce anything very much more dangerous.

*Winston Churchill, in 1939*

## ODDS

Every person now living in the United States has one chance out of fourteen of dying of tuberculosis and one chance in fifty of becoming affected with this disease.

*Dr Linsly R Williams, then Managing Director of National Tuberculosis Association, quoted in the* Congressional Record

## OIL PIPELINES

The caribou love it. They rub against it and they have babies. There are more caribou in Alaska than you can shake a stick at.

*George Bush, then Vice-President, on the Alaska pipeline*

## OIL RIGS

It isn't as if you were looking at the ocean through a little frame and now somebody put something in the way.

*Ronald Reagan, on why offshore oil rigs shouldn't bother anybody*

## Old-fashioned American virtues

I'm one of those who sort of vacillates as we can afford to vacillate. My bend toward conservatism is purely and simply based on ... economic circumstances ... It may be that, by the next campaign, circumstances would be somewhat better and it may be that I would be somewhat more liberal.

*Congressman Ike Andrews*

## Oliver North

He had the love and respect of everyone who worked for or with him. He knew what he wanted and how to get it. He possessed great charm and wit and was, it is said, the first man to bring real humour and fun to the White House since Kennedy.

*Actor David Keith, on Oliver North, whom he played on a TV mini-series*

## Omissions

It will be noticed that some omissions will appear in this edition.

*Thomas Carlyle, Victorian essayist, historian, critic and social commentator, in the opening of his famous* Oliver Cromwell

## Opposites

I told you to make one longer than another, and instead you have made one shorter than the other – the opposite.

*Sir Boyle Roche*

## Orders

Sit down and go out.

*Mayor of Birmingham, Alabama, to an unruly council member*

Outlawing killing, murder, assassination:

I suppose [we could have one], but the actual writing of a statute might be a little difficult.

*CIA Director William Colby, on congressional suggestions for a law barring political assassinations*

## Over-eagerness

I happen to be a Republican President, ah, the Vice-President.

*Dan Quayle while stumping for Republican candidates*

## Overpopulation

Heaven is a place large enough to accommodate 299,900,000,000,000 souls with a mansion of 100 rooms each, 16 x 16 x 16.

*Revd Dr W Graham Walker, speaking at the Highland Street Christian Church, Memphis, Tennessee, 1926*

120

## OXYGEN

Folks, this is perfect weather for today's game. Not a breath of air.

*Curt Gowdy, network sports announcer, on air*

## PEOPLE

To hell with the public! I'm here to represent the people!

*New Jersey State Senator*

The 37 fellows (of the Royal University) are divided into 29 fellows and 8 medical fellows. Half of these 29 fellows are attached to the University College . . . The other half of the 29 fellows are distributed over the country.

*Michael McCarthy, in his book* Priests and People

## PERSONAL BANKING

It won't be long before customers should be able to complete most of their banking transactions without any personal contact. This will enable banks to offer more personal contact.

Credit and Financial Management Magazine, *1976, predicting the future of banking*

## Personal Choice

One problem that we've had even in the best of times . . . is the people who are sleeping on the grates. The homeless who are homeless, you might say, by choice.

*President Ronald Reagan, on* Good Morning America, *31 January 1984*

## Personality

Some quiet guys are inwardly outgoing.

*Ralph Kiner, Mets broadcaster*

## Personal Touch

Nothing could be more personal than a tape.

*Julie Nixon Eisenhower*

## Pesticides

Sure, it's going to kill a lot of people, but they may be dying of something else anyway.

*Othal Brand, member of a Texas pesticide review board, on chlordane*

## Philosophy

Beauty is love made real, and the spirit of love is God. And the state of beauty, love and God is happiness. A transcendent state of beauty, love and God is peace. Peace and love is a state of beauty, love and God. One is an active state of happiness and the other is a transcendent state. That's peace.



*Imelda Marcos, campaigning for her husband, Ferdinand Marcos, then Philippine President*

## Photographs

That picture was taken out of context.

*Jeff Innis, New York Mets pitcher, on a bad picture taken of him*

## Physics

In no way is it possible for a person to be in two places at the same time, especially if there is a great distance in between.

*Judge Amado Guerrero, Mexican Tenth District Federal Court, on a defendant's alibi*

## Pistols

Mr John Burns held a pistol at their heads, but now it had come home to roost.

*Overheard during English parliamentary debate*

## Pliers

They're multipurpose. Not only do they put the clips on, but they take them off.

*Pratt & Whitney spokesperson explaining why the company charged the Air Force nearly $1,000 for a pair of pliers*

## Pockets

If you put the honourable member on an uninhabited island they would not be there twenty-four hours before they had their hands in the pockets of the naked savages.

*Unnamed politician, overheard during a debate*

## Poetry

The style is clitoral, as far as I'm concerned.

*Professor Paula Bennett, of the Department of Humanities and Social Science, Seattle Central Community College*

## Police

Get the thing straight once and for all. The policeman isn't there to create disorder. The policeman is there to preserve disorder.

*Richard Daley, Mayor of Chicago*

## Politics

We move to Camp David and hide. They can't get in there.

*H R Haldeman, White House Chief of Staff, on the Watergate tapes, suggesting how they could avoid subpoenas*

. . . let's assume that . . . a disaster should occur. Let's assume that an airplane drops out of – or under – both of the people we're talking about, both Ford and Reagan. Let's assume that, if you want to assume a macabre situation, then I might do it.

*John Connally, ex-Republican presidential candidate in the 1980 campaign, explaining to Barbara Walters what it would take for him to re-enter the race*

WATER MONDALE (Democratic candidate): George Bush doesn't have the manhood to apologize.

GEORGE BUSH (Republican candidate): Well, on the manhood thing, I'll put mine up against his any time.

By golly, what do you suppose is behind that?

*Ronald Reagan, when told about an attack on Iraq by Israeli fighters*

I hope I stand for anti-bigotry, anti-Semitism, anti-racism. This is what drives me.

*George Bush in 1988 when aides accused of anti-Semitism resigned from his campaign*

We are in favour of a law which absolutely prohibits the sale of liquor on Sunday, but we are against its enforcement.

*1920s Democratic platform in Syracuse (as a result of being caught between the saloon and anti-saloon forces)*

Politics makes strange bedclothes.

*Rosalind Russell, 40s' and 50s' movie star*

## Pollution

Approximately 80 per cent of our air pollution stems from hydrocarbons released by vegetation, so let's not go overboard in setting and enforcing tough emission standards from man-made sources.

*President Ronald Reagan*

I've always thought that under-populated countries in Africa are vastly under-populated.

*Lawrence Summers, chief economist of the World Bank, explaining why we should export toxic wastes to Third World countries*

America's lands may be ravaged as a result of the actions of the environmentalists.

*James Watt, Secretary of the Interior under Reagan*

## Poor People

Sometimes [they] don't smell too good, so love can have no nose.

*Evangelist wife, Tammy Faye Bakker, preaching about the poor*

## Popularity

Nobody goes there anymore. It's too crowded.

*Yogi Berra, explaining why he didn't want to go to dinner at a particular restaurant*

## Posterity

By posterity, sir, I do not mean our ancestors, but those who are to come immediately after them.

*Sir Boyle Roche, correcting himself*

## Poultry Inspectors

The crime bill passed by the Senate would reinstate the Federal death penalty for certain violent crimes: assassinating the President; hijacking an airliner, and murdering a Government poultry inspector.

*Knight Ridder News Service dispatch*

## Poverty

The poor don't need gas because they're not working.

*California Senator S I Hayakawa, explaining why we shouldn't worry about the effect on the poor if gas prices rose several dollars a gallon*

The elderly eat less.

*California Senator S I Hayakawa, explaining why the elderly don't need a special exemption on food stamp eligibility*

He's living beyond his means, but he can afford it.

*Movie mogul, Samuel Goldwyn*

Mr Thornton Burke gave a terrible picture of life in the East End of London, where he said there were thousands of people grinding their faces in the dust of poverty and trying at the same time to keep their heads above water.

*From a brochure by an advertising group in London*

Low earnings seem to be the key reason why someone who usually works full time is a member of a poor family.

*US Bureau of Labor Statistics (conclusions of a study detailing poverty in America)*

## Prayers

May the word of the Lord be as a nail driven in a sure place, sending its roots downwards and its branches upwards.

*Prayer by a clergyman*

## Precipices and Cliffs

You are standing on the edge of a precipice that will be a weight on your necks all the rest of your life.

*Statement by member of Dublin Corporation*

## Precognition

There will be a procession next Sunday afternoon in the grounds of the Monastery; but if it rains in the afternoon, the procession will take place in the morning.

*From a statement read to a church congregation*

## Predictions



They couldn't hit an elephant at this dist–

*General John Sedgwick, Union commander in the Civil War, speaking his last words as he was watching enemy troops during the Battle of Spotsylvania Court House*

Once we have got a Republic it is for you and me to have such a party formed in Ireland that we may take the machinery in our hands, and making the road level go forward uphill to make the new horizon.

*Dublin labour leader, late nineteenth century*

## Presidency

The President is guilty of misdemeanours. It is inherent in the office.

*Leonard Garment, special White House consultant, on then President Richard Nixon's involvement in Watergate*

Now I'm no cowboy. I pitch horseshoes for a living, but I don't ride these broncos.

*George Bush in Texas, explaining what his job as President entailed*

I am now going over and sign, and as you can notice how cold it is, twelve pens there are too cold–they can only sign one letter, each pen. If my name came out to thirteen letters, I would have misspelled it.

*President Ronald Reagan at the signing ceremony of a Social Security bill*

I wouldn't want anything to happen to the President of the United States even though I might be in some kind of line of succession. It probably will never happen, but it's nice to think about anyway.

*Senator Warren Magnuson, upon becoming president pro tem of the Senate*

## Press Agents

[You reporters] should have printed what he meant, not what he said.

*Earl Bush, press aide to Chicago Mayor Richard Daley, Sr, scolding reporters*

## Principles

I will talk to my stockbroker, and unless he gives me some good reason why I shouldn't, I would be pleased to dispose [my South African investments]. I am very much opposed to apartheid.

*California State Senator Milton Marks, on his South African stockholdings; in the* Los Angeles Times

## Priorities

Here at the ministry we have other, more urgent, situations to deal with.

*Jorge Luna of the Peruvian Labour Ministry after hearing that gold miners in the jungle were enslaving thousands of children*

## Problems

Everyone wants to jump into my throat!

*Michael Curtiz, Hollywood director, complaining to his assistant*

## Profits

The profits shall be divided and the residue goes to the governor.

*Irish Bank Bill of 1808*

## Promises

I have not reneged on my promise. I have changed my mind.

*New York gubernatorial candidate Pierre Rinfret, on why he released only one of the tax returns he had promised to show the public*

## Publishing

Send all the details. Never mind the facts.

*Telegram from the editor of the old* New York World *to his Washington correspondent*

## Qualifications

After finding no qualified candidates for the position of principal, the school department is extremely pleased to announce the appointment of David Steele to the post.

*Philip Streifer, superintendent of schools, Barrington, Rhode Island*

Anyone can be elected governor. I'm proof of that.

*Joe Frank Harris, two-term Georgia governor, talking about who might fill his shoes*

## Questions

If you ask me anything I don't know, I'm not going to answer.

*Yogi Berra to a radio broadcaster before an interview*

In a general way, we try to anticipate some of your questions so that I can respond 'no comment' with some degree of knowledge.

*William Baker, CIA spokesman, to the press*

Have we gone beyond the bounds of reasonable dishonesty?

*CIA memo; introduced during the Westmoreland/CBS libel suit*

## Quiet

If you can't keep quiet, shut up!

*Gregory Ratoff, 30s' and 40s' Hollywood director of films such as* Intermezzo, *to his crew*

I want to hear it so quiet we can hear a mouse dropping.

*Gregory Ratoff*

After being told the correct metaphor for quiet was a pin:

Exactly, like a mouse pin dropping.

*Gregory Ratoff*

## Quotes

I really didn't say everything I said.

*Yogi Berra, in* The Sporting News, *discussing the sayings he has become famous for*

Don't quote what he says. Say what he means!

*Campaign aide for Senator Barry Goldwater, then making a bid for the 1964 presidency, to reporters*

## Race Relations

Sure, I look like a white man. But my heart is as black as anyone's here.

*George Wallace, Alabama governor and then presidential candidate, during a campaign speech to a largely black audience*

Why would we have different races if God meant us to be alike and associate with each other?

*Lester Maddox, former governor of Georgia*

## Radioactive Leaks

The thing is this – we have incidents happening here all the time.

*Department of Energy spokesman at Hanford, Washington, on why no announcement was made on a leak of radioactive material*

## Rape

I say this a lot, and I probably shouldn't: the difference between rape and seduction is salesmanship.

*Bill Carpenter, Mayor of Independence, Missouri*

## Rats

I smell a rat, I see him floating in the air, but mark me, I shall nip him in the bud.

*Sir Boyle Roche, eighteenth-century MP from Tralee and famous word mangler*

## Reading the Crowd

They made an animal-type grunting sound when the National Guard was mentioned. There were some good-natured grunts. Let me admit theoretically that some people hissed.

*David Beckwith, press secretary to Vice-President Dan Quayle, commenting on rumours that West Point cadets hissed at Quayle*

## Ronald Reagan

If I listened to him [Michael Dukakis] long enough I would be convinced that we're in an economic downturn and people are homeless and going without food and medical attention and that we've got to do something about the unemployed.

*President Ronald Reagan, during the presidential campaign, talking about Democratic candidate Michael Dukakis's criticism of the Administration*

My fellow Americans. I've signed legislation that will outlaw Russia forever. We begin bombing in five minutes.

*President Ronald Reagan, before he was going to make a radio broadcast unaware that the mike was already on*

## REBUKES

Sir, you have tasted two whole worms; you have hissed all my mystery lectures and been caught fighting a liar in the quad, you will leave Oxford by the next town drain.

*Revd William A Spooner telling a student to leave his class for non-attendance and lighting fires; his classic spoonerism*

## RECORD EXECUTIVES

You'll never make it – four groups are out. Go back to Liverpool . . .

*Decca Record executives to the Beatles in 1962*

## REDUNDANCY

I'm for abolishing and doing away with redundancy.

*J Curtis McKay of the Wisconsin State Elections Board*

## REFORM

We must restore to Chicago all the good things it never had.

*Richard Daley, Mayor of Chicago*

To those who say it is time to reform this organization and that it's time the officers stopped selling out its members, I say, 'Go to hell.'

*Frank Fitzsimmons, Teamsters Union President*

## Relatives

This extraordinary man left no children behind him, except his brother, who was killed at the same time.

*From a biography of French revolutionary leader Robespierre, in a nineteenth-century Irish newspaper*

My dear Sandby. I'm glad to see you. Pray is it you or your brother?

*Sir W Caulfield, British literary figure, greeting a friend*

## Religion

It isn't like I came down from Mount Sinai with the tabloids.

*Indianapolis Colts coach Ron Meyer*

## Repeating Yourself

I have reiterated over again what I have said before.

*Mayor Robert F Wagner of New York*

## Retreat

Should the Red hordes continue to pour across the Yalu, it might not only render impossible the resumption of our offensive, but conceivably could eventuate in a movement in retrograde.

*General Douglas MacArthur in a press conference, commenting on the situation in Korea*

## Revolutions

I would take my own head by the hair, cut it off, and presenting it to the despot, would say to him, 'Tyrant, behold the act of a free man.'

*A perhaps over-zealous French revolutionary speaking to a mob in Paris in 1789, reported by Anglo-American revolutionary Thomas Paine*

## Rhythm Method, according to experts

. . . the safe times [for sex] are the week before and the week of ovulation.

*Dr Ruth Westheimer, in* First Love: A Young People's Guide to Sexual Information. *The typo ('safe' for 'unsafe') resulted in a huge book recall, and a new corrected edition*

## Riding

Now ride off in all directions.

*Michael Curtiz, directed Gary Cooper on a horse*

## Right, being

You are partly one hundred per cent right.

*Movie mogul, Samuel Goldwyn*

## Riots

. . . airplanes may be used for the purpose of keeping rioters off roofs by means of machine gun fire . . . infantry should and will invariably constitute the major part of any command employed in suppressing domestic disorders . . . armoured cars will be especially valuable in riot duty . . .

*General Douglas MacArthur, Military Aid in Disturbances (1935), in which he also comes out against the use of blanks, as an 'admission of weakness'. Shoot to kill, he urged. From George Seldes, famous muckraking journalist of the era*

## Roles

It's a great role and you'll play it to the tilt.

*Gregory Ratoff*

## Roosevelt, Franklin

I'm not trying to compare myself with Roosevelt, but he couldn't walk either.

*George Wallace, campaigning in the 1976 presidential race*

## Ropes

Those who vote for this bond issue will be putting a rope around their necks which will suck at their vitals like a deadly vampire.

*Overheard during congressional debate*

## Running

I'm very sorry, but I ran like a fire hydrant.

*Michael Curtiz, Hollywood director, apologizing for being late to an appointment*

In all other respects, he's done a very good job.

*Press officer, Noel Jones, of the British Embassy in Moscow, commenting on Konstantin Demakhin, embassy driver for nineteen years, who, after the collapse of the Soviet Union, announced that he had been a KGB spy*

## Salaries

People think we make $3 million and $4 million a year. They don't realize that most of us only make $500,000.

*Baseball player, Pete Incaviglia*

## Salvation

It was necessary to destroy the village in order to save it.

*American officer in Vietnam in a 1968 report on the razing of Vietnamese village, Ben Tre*

## Samoans

You all look like happy campers to me. Happy campers you are, happy campers you have been, and as far as I am concerned, happy campers you will always be.

*Vice-President, Dan Quayle, addressing a group of Samoans during a Pacific trip*

No 1, to determine what it is, at different age and ability levels, that children ought to know, believing that we can never determine if children know what they ought to know if we haven't determined what it is we think they ought to know.

*Kentucky Governor Wallace Wilkinson on his education reform package, in the 70s*

## SCREENPLAYS

You call this a script? Give me a couple of $5,000-a-week writers and I'll write it myself.

*Producer, Joe Pasternak*

## SEEDS

God hath kindled a seed in this nation.

*Oliver Cromwell, seventeenth-century Lord Protector of England, in a famous address to the nation*

## SEEING

I saw no corn standing in ricks, a thing I never saw before and would not have believed it had I not seen it.

*William Cobbett, late eighteenth- and early nineteenth-century English writer and champion of the poor, in his most famous book,* Rural Rides

## Segues

If you think the football game was exciting, wait until you hear the report from Tom Aspell from Amman, Jordan.

*Tom Brokaw, NBC News anchorman, just after the NFL game had been broadcast, in his lead-in to the story about the Gulf War*

## Sermons

We often pursue the shadow until the bubble bursts and leaves nothing but the ashes in our hands.

*From a sermon by a British clergyman*

## Servants

We have spoken of that sanguinary year, 1973. In those troubled times it was that French domestics set an example of the greatest devotion. There were many even who, rather than betray their masters, allowed themselves to be guillotined in their place, and when, when happier days returned, silently and respectfully went back to their work.

*Le Figaro, Paris, February 1890; from an essay on home life during the French Revolution*

## Sex

Making love is a mental illness that wastes time and energy.

*People's Republic of China, official Communist Party proclamation, 1971*

Sex will outlive us all.

*Movie mogul, Samuel Goldwyn*

Sexual orientation is against everything in this book [said while waving a Bible].

*Robert Shaw, Chicago alderman, in a city council debate on gay rights*

Letter from A M, McW to *Watertown* (New York) *Daily Times*: Is it possible for a doctor to determine the sex of an unborn child by listening to the foetal heartbeat? (A M, McW)

ANSWER: No. In any case, anybody's guess is as likely to be right as wrong. About half of all babies are boys or girls.

Ladies, without distinction of sex, would be welcome.

*From a handbill for a political demonstration in the early 1900s*

My sister's expecting a baby, and I don't know if I'm going to be an uncle or an aunt.

*Chuck Nevitt, basketball player at North Carolina State University, as reported in* Sports Illustrated

The Great Synod of 1920 will always be memorable for having at length admitted women to be enrolled in the list of registered vestry men.

*The Very Revd Dr Ross, speaking about the Tuam Diocesan Synod*

I don't know. They were wearing a paper bag over their head.

*Yogi Berra after he had seen a streaker and was asked if the person was male or female*

As poet, actress, literary critic and artist, Mrs Wyatt Cooper, better known as Gloria Vanderbilt, has often been called an up-to-date and very feminine version of the many-faceted Renaissance man.

*A* Life *magazine staff writer in the introduction to a series of photos of Gloria Vanderbilt (4 October 1968)*

You should hear her sing. She's a female Lena Horne.

*Producer, Joe Pasternak*

## Sexual Harassment

Sexual harassment on the job is not a problem for virtuous women.

*Phyllis Schlafly, conservative activist and founder of the Eagle Forum*

## Sexual Preferences

We're well aware of the male homosexual problem in this country, which is of course minor, but to our certain knowledge there is not one lesbian in England.

*Lord Chamberlain of England to Lillian Hellman during a discussion of the play* The Children's Hour *(from* Lilly *by Peter Feibleman)*

## Shakespeare, Little-known facts

Quite a number of people also describe the German classical author, Shakespeare, as belonging to the English literature, because – quite accidentally born at Stratford-on-Avon – he was forced by authorities of that country to write in English.

*From the* Deutscher Weckruf und Beobachter, *1940*

I asked one of the principal actors of the dramatic theatre about Shakespeare, and he told me that he is just learning German, so that he may soon be able to read Shakespeare in the original.

*From the Soviet literary magazine* Literaturnaya Gazeta, *1940*

Shakespeare has not only shown human nature as it is, but as it would be found in situations to which it cannot be exposed.

*Samuel Johnson, great eighteenth-century English writer*

## Shoes

My shoes are size 2½ – the same size as my feet.

*Elaine Page*

I've got ten pairs of training shoes, one for every day of the week.

*Samantha Fox*

I never put on a pair of shoes until I've worn them five years.

*Movie mogul, Samuel Goldwyn*

A tax on leather would press heavily on the bare-footed peasantry of Ireland.

*Crofton Moore Vandeleur, British statesman*

## Silence

Lead us in a few words of silent prayer.

*Ex-Houston Oiler and Florida State coach Bill Peterson*

## Singing Style

They were singing without accompaniment. You know – acapulco.

*Director, Gregory Ratoff, telling of hearing a singing group*

## Sleep

The best cure for insomnia is to get a lot of sleep.

*Attributed to Senator S I Hayakawa*

I usually take a two-hour nap, from one o'clock to four.

*Yogi Berra, explaining what he does before night games*

## Sleeves

The time has come to strip to the waist and tuck up our shirt sleeves.

*Overheard during political debate*

## Smokescreens

I didn't inhale.

*Bill Clinton, as Democratic presidential candidate, answering rumours that he had smoked marijuana*

## Solidity

We appeal down to the fundamental principles which underlie the tossing waves on the surface.

*Former Archbishop of Canterbury, in speech in House of Lords*

## Space Exploration

Mars is essentially in the same orbit. Mars is somewhat the same distance from the sun, which is very important. We have seen pictures where there are canals, we believe, and water. If there is water, that means there is oxygen. If oxygen, that means we can breathe.

*Vice-President Dan Quayle*

Space travel is utter bilge.

*Sir Richard Woolley, 50s' Astronomer Royal of Britain, predicting the likelihood of space travel*

I think space exploration is very important and can yield a lot of knowledge.

*Contestant for Mr New Jersey Male, when asked what he would do with a million dollars*

## Speaking

Mr Speaker, if I had said that I would not have been allowed to.

*Anonymous speaker during British parliamentary debate*

I am not going to trouble the House further than to express my unutterable disgust at the way in which I have been treated.

*John O'Conner MP in Houses of Commons, 1907*

## Speech

Ladies and gentlemen, if this coercion measure is passed no man in Ireland will be able to speak upon politics unless he is born deaf and dumb.

*Lord Charles Russell, Liberal MP, in an 1880 speech*

Having a speech writer would definitely be too plastic. I just try to remember six key words before every talk.

*Mark Spitz, swimmer and Olympic gold medalist, on whether or not he had people write his speeches for him*

Ladies and gentlemen, it is a great pleasure to be with you today. For immediate release only.

*New Mexico Senator, Joe Montoya, at a dinner speech in Albuquerque. He had rushed in late and read straight from his press release*

## Spelling

Mr Speaker, this bill is a phony with a capital F.

*Congressman during a heated congressional debate*

## Spontaneity

[It was a ] semi-planned spontaneous stop.

*Douglas Scamman, 1992 Bush New Hampshire presidential campaign manager, on a staged campaign stop at a farm*

## Sports

Baseball is 90 per cent mental. The other half is physical.

*Yogi Berra*

Now Juantorena opens his legs – and really shows his class.

*David Coleman, broadcaster at the 1976 Montreal Olympics*

## Stamp Collecting

Down with the greedy Stamp Bourgeoisie! Long LIve the Red Philatelic International, leader and guardian of the world's working class philatelists and numismatists! Proletarian stamp and coin collectors, Unite!

*From the front page of the 1924 Russian magazine for stamp collectors,* Red Philatelist. *This manifesto was published in English, French, German and Russian*

## Stars

I looked at all the superstars. What is their different thing? Their hair . . . I wanted to be a star. I said, 'I have to fix my hair.'

*Rob Pilatus, one half of Grammy-winning group Milli Vanilli, who were later fond to be lip-synching to pre-recorded songs sung by other singers, commenting on his $700 hairstyle*

## Statistics

These are not my figures I'm quoting. They're from someone who knows what he's talking about.

*Congressman in debate*

## Statuary

Frances has the most beautiful hands in the world, and someday I'm going to make a bust of them.

*Movie mogul, Samuel Goldwyn*

## Stones

The very recognition of these or any of them by the jurisprudence of a nation is a mortal wound to the very keystone upon which the whole vast arch of morality reposes.

*Thomas De Quincey, nineteenth-century English essayist, author of* Confessions of an English Opium-Eater

## Strangers

What do you mean, stranger? I don't even know you.

*Michael Curtiz, director, to a man on the Warner Brothers movie lot who greeted him with a 'Howdy, stranger'*

## Strategic Defence Initiative

I don't think the American public wants to be bothered with the what, when, and how of lasers in space and things like that. Whether the technology will work or how much it will cost – these are peripheral arguments.

*Rick Sellers, executive director of the Coalition for the SDI, as quoted in the* Washington Post

## Strength

Gil Hodges is so strong he could snap your earbrows off.

*Casey Stengel, famed manager of the New York Yankees and Mets*

## Strikes

I still feel that the best answer is a head-on-head, man-to-man negotiation between the union and the airline.

*President George Bush during the 1989 Eastern Airline's pilots' strike*

## Suicide

The only way to stop this suicide wave is to make it a capital offence, punishable by death.

*Irish legislator in Parliament*

## Sunshine

I selected a shady nook and basked in the sunshine.

*R J Mecredy, writer and publisher, describing a day during his summer vacation*

## Superlatives

It's more than magnificent. It's mediocre!

*Attributed to Samuel Goldwyn, movie mogul*

## Suprises

This is a delightful surprise to the extent that it is a surprise and it is only a surprise to the extent that we anticipated.

*James Baker, Secretary of State, discussing administration reaction to the Kohl/Gorbachev German reunification agreement*

## Swords

I will draw my sword from the hilt, and will not cease firing until I have proved every statement true.

*Speaker at a Walthamstown town council meeting*

The problems will be explained to the people which I think the people are interested in. I said the explanations will be given to the people in the problems I think concerns them.

*Chicago Mayor Richard Daley, Sr*

## Taking a Stand

I am philosophically opposed to any fare increase . . . That does not mean I will not support one.

*Fairfax County, Virginia, Supervisor Joseph Alexander*

## Talking

It was hard to have a conversation with anyone, there were so many people talking.

*Yogi Berra, talking about a dinner at the White House*

I'm not going to discuss what I'm going to bring up . . . Even if I don't discuss it, I'm not going to discuss it.

*President George Bush, talking about his relationship with the press*

He got me by the throat so that I could not speak and I asked him several times to let me go.

*Victim testifying during an assault case*

There is a great deal more I want to say, but I don't want to say any more, and I won't.

*Delegate to the National Association for the Prevention of Consumption, Manchester*

## Tape Erasures

Some sinister force had come in and applied the other energy source and taken care of the information on the tape.

*Alexander Haig, giving his theory on the 181/2-minute gap in the Nixon tapes to Special Judge John Sirica*

## Taste

I want this house over-furnished in perfect taste.

*Michael Curtiz, director, talking about a set design*

Well, David, did you do any fornicating this weekend?

*Richard Nixon to David Frost before an interview*

## Taxation

If a third or more of our population were killed in an attack (a conservative estimate by the standards of the Rand Corporation's 'Study of Non-military Defense') a stronger estate tax would have tremendous revenue potential.

*From a 1963 Federal Reserve System planning document*

## Taxes

Sure, some people pay money they many not owe. We make mistakes.

*IRS Commissioner Fred Goldberg, Jr, responding to a magazine article that reported IRS billing errors of $7-15 billion*

Only the little people pay taxes.

*Leona Helmsley, hotel manager, who was later indicted for non-payment of taxes*

## TEACHERS, INFALLIBILITY OF

He has never learned anything, and he can do nothing in decent style.

*Johann Georg Albrechtsberger, composer, theoretician, and one of Ludwig van Beethoven's teachers*

It doesn't matter what he does, he will never amount to anything.

*One of Albert Einstein's teachers, giving his opinion on Einstein's future to Einstein's father*

[He is] over-age and certain to prove mediocre.

*Francesco Basily, principal of the Royal and Imperial Conservatory of Milan, rejecting the application of composer/musician Giuseppe Verdi to study at the Conservatory*

## TELEPHONE INSTRUCTIONS

TO SPEAK TO A GUEST IN ANOTHER ROOM: Please follow these instructions: 1st Floor – add 250 to the room number and dial, on the 2nd, 3rd and 4th Floors – dial the number required. 5th Floor – subtract 250 from the room number and dial, eg to contact Room 510 dial 260 EXCEPT for Room 542 whose number is 294.

*Telephone instructions posted in the Zimbabwe Sun Hotel, as reported in the* Far Eastern Economic Review

## Telephones

The telephone company is urging people to please not use the telephone unless it is absolutely necessary in order to keep the lines open for emergency personnel. We'll be right back after this break to give away a pair of Phil Collins' concert tickets to caller number 95.

*A Los Angeles radio DJ shortly after the February 1990 earthquake*

Federal Bureau of Investigation (718) 459-3140

If No Answer Call (718) 459-3140

*Nassau County NYNEX Telephone Directory (1991) Listing*

## Telephone Wires

. . . the number of new overhead wires would be comparatively small, and would be placed underground.

*Postmaster General, during debate explaining ease of a re-wiring project*

## Telling it like it is

Telling it like it is means telling it like it was and how it is now that it isn't what it was to the is now people.

*Jill Johnston, in* Village Voice

## Thoughts

As I was sitting on my seat, a thought struck me.

*From a maiden congressional speech, as reported by Massachusetts State Senator John F Parker*

## Time

The time is here, and rapidly approaching.

*William Field, MP*

## Time Passing

We've all passed a lot of water since then.

*Attributed to an old Hollywood producer, reminiscing about one of his first films*

We want to minimize as much as possible the impact on the lives of the people who live in Marin County – and at that hour, there's not that much traffic.

*San Quentin warden, explaining why he set the execution time for Robert Alton Harris at 3am*

## Tooch Dirt, removing

Pull another end of gross and put along the ditch gap of bow-finger and turn up to get down along another bow-finger then return to button on the centre.

*Directions from a Japanese tooth flosser (grosser), with the accompanying motto: 'Help you use gross smoothly and clean tooch dirt', reported in* Far Eastern Economic Review

## Top Hits

'Indignantly Condemn the Wang-Chan-Chiang-Yao Gang of Four'

*Hit song of 1976, according to the* People's Daily, *Beijing, China*

## Tourism

Come to think of it, why wait until May to visit Memphis? April is the month the Reverend Martin Luther King Jr was assassinated in the city.

*From an item in* USA Today

## Trade Deficit

[After a nuclear attack] . . . so far as the balance of payments is concerned, our results show exports consistently exceeding imports by amounts varying from about 150 to 200 per cent.

*Two economists speaking at a Fort Monroe, Virginia, seminar sponsored by Civil Defense in 1967*

## Translations

Equal goes is loose.

*German President Heinrich Lubke, translating 'It will soon begin' (Gleich geht es los) into English*

Pepsi brings your ancestors back from the grave.

*Ad slogan 'Pepsi Comes Alive' as initially translated into Chinese*

We pray for MacArthur's erection.

*Sign supposedly erected by Japanese citizens in Tokyo, when General MacArthur was considering a run for United States President*

I desire the Poles carnally.

*President Jimmy Carter's mistranslation in a 1977 speech in Poland*

1. At the rise of the hand of the policeman, stop rapidly. Do not pass him or otherwise disrespect him.

2. If pedestrian obstacle your path, tootle horn melodiously. If he continue to obstacle, tootle horn vigorously and utter vocal warning such as 'Hi, Hi'.

3. If wandering horse by roadside obstacle your path, beware that he do not take fright as you pass him. Go soothingly by, or stop by roadside till he pass away.

4. If road mope obstacle your path, refrain from pass on hill or round curve. Follow patiently till road arrive at straight level stretch. Then tootle horn melodiously and stop on, passing at left and waving hand courteously to honourable road mope in passing.

5. Beware of greasy corner where lurk skid demon. Cease step on, approach slowly, round cautiously, resume step on gradually.

*From an official Japanese guide for English-speaking drivers, 1936*

## TRANSPORTATION

When two trains approach each other at a crossing, they shall both come to a full stop and neither shall start up until the other has gone.

*A law in Kansas*

## Trees

A tree's a tree. How many more do you need to look at?

*President Ronald Reagan*

There is today in the United States as much forest as there was when Washington was at Valley Forge.

*President Ronald Reagan*

When you see one redwood, you've seen them all.

*President Ronald Reagan*

## Trees, Second Thoughts

I don't believe a tree is a tree and if you've seen one you've seen them all.

*President Ronald Reagan*

## Tributes

A real lady who has given unwittingly of her philosophy to the nation.

*President Gerald Ford on adviser Ann Armstrong*

## Troubles

Remember Lincoln, going to his knees in times of trial in the Civil War and all that stuff. You can't be. And we are blessed. So don't feel sorry for – don't cry for me, Argentina.

*President George Bush, in his 15 January 1992 New Hampshire campaign speech*

## Trustworthiness

That fellow is a crook. His word isn't worth the paper it's written on.

*Attributed to movie mogul, Samuel Goldwyn*

## Truth

I don't want to tell you any half-truths unless they're completely accurate.

*Dennis Rappaport, boxing manager, explaining his silence regarding boxer, Thomas Hearns*

There are two kinds of truth. There are real truths and there are made-up truths.

*Marion Barry, Mayor of Washington DC, on his arrest for drug use*

If I told you the truth, I'd be a hypocrite.

*Michael Curtiz, Hollywood director, when asked his opinion of a producer*

The honourable member did not want the truth; the honourable member had asked for facts.

*Joseph Chamberlain, nineteenth-century British statesman and leader of the Liberal Unionists*

## Twentieth-Century, observations

[The Holocaust] was an obscene period in our nation's history . . . this century's history . . . We all lived in this century, I didn't live in this century.

*Dan Quayle, then Indiana senator and Republican vice-presidential candidate, during a new conference in which he was asked his opinion about the Holocaust*

## Twenty-Twenty Hindsight

You know, I've always wondered about the taping equipment. But I'm damn glad we have it.

*President Richard Nixon to White House aide*

## Typesetting, Great Moments in

Several of the Revd Dr Mudge's friends called upon him yesterday, and after a conversation the unsuspecting pig was seized by the hind leg, and slid along a beam until he reached the hot-water tank . . . Thereupon he came forward and said that there were times when the feelings overpowered one, and for that reason he would not attempt to do more than thank those around him for the manner in which such a huge animal was cut into fragments was simply astonishing. The doctor concluded his remarks, when the machine seized him and in less time than it takes to write it the pig was cut into fragments and worked up into delicious sausage. The occasion will be long remembered by the doctor's friends as one of the most delightful of their lives. The best prices can be procured for tenpence a pound, and we are sure that those who have sat so long under his ministry will rejoice that he has been treated so handsomely.

*From an English newspaper in the late 1880s, when two stories – one on a patent pig-killing and sausage-making machine and the other on the Revd Dr Mudge being presented with a gold-headed cane – were mistakenly pieced together by typographers*

## US History

[Students and their ancestors] have been coming to the land now called the United States for millennia.

*A City University of New York professor in a newsletter*

## Unanimity

Resolved unanimously with one dissenting voice.

*From the report of an Irish Board of Guardians meeting*

## Uncertainty

There's a lot of uncertainty that's not clear in my mind.

*Gib Lewis, Speaker of the Texas House*

## Understatements

The fact that my father was President and Chief Justice of the United States was a tremendous help and inspiration in my public career.

*Senator Robert A Taft, son of President William H Taft*

A lot of guys said it was fate that stopped it. Probably I would have been dead if it went over.

*Dave Munday, stuntsperson and daredevil, after the foam-padded barrel he was in caught on a crag inches away from the edge of Niagara Falls*

RON ZIEGLER: So it was a really terrific year except for the downside.

QUESTIONER: What downside?

ZIEGLER: Watergate.

*Press Secretary Ron Ziegler when asked about the accomplishments of the Nixon administration*

The country is not in good condition.

*Calvin Coolidge, ex-President, sharing his erudite opinion on the Great Depression in January 1931*

## UNEMPLOYMENT

It [unemployment insurance] provides pre-paid vacations for a segment of our country which has made it a way of life.

*President Ronald Reagan*

Now we are trying to get unemployment to go up and I think we're going to succeed.

*President Ronald Reagan at a 1982 GOP fund raiser*

The right to suffer is one of the joys of a free economy.

*Howard Pyle, aide to President Eisenhower, commenting on the unemployment situation in Detroit*

When a great many people are unable to find work, unemployment results.

*Calvin Coolidge, ex-President, discussing the United States economic situation in 1931*

## Uniforms

There's someone warming up in the bull pen, but he's obscured by his number.

*Jerry Coleman, San Diego Padres announcer*

## Unknowns

We received yesterday morning from an unknown source whose immense generosity is well-known to us . . .

*Leon Daudet, French royalist leader, speaking about a large amount of money received by his Royalist Party*

## Urban Centres

Bison, elk and puma are now extinct in the city of Macon.

*A report sponsored by the Federal Writers' Project, Georgia, 1936*

## Verbs

I've asked Bill. I've said, 'Bill, work the problem.'

*President George Bush about drug czar William Bennett's job*

You'd better caveat that statement.

*Alexander Haig, then Secretary of State*

I would like the government to do all it can to mitigate, then, in understanding, in mutuality of interest, in concern for the common good, our tasks will be solved.

*President Warren G Harding, trying to make a point about the government's role, as quoted in H L Mencken's essay 'Gamalielese'. Mencken coined the term 'Gamalielese' (based on Harding's middle name, Gamaliel) to refer to Harding's pretentious way of speaking*

## Vietnam Vets

No wonder we lost the war.

*Dubious quip by Dorchester, Massachusetts, Judge Paul King, to a Vietnam vet appearing before him*

## Violence, the CIA

I have definitional problems with the word 'violence'. I don't know what the word 'violence' means.

*William Colby, Director of the CIA*

## Virility

We're finally going to wrassle to the ground this giant orgasm that is just out of control.

*Arizona Senator, Dennis DeConcini on a balanced budget amendment*

It takes a virile man to make a chicken pregnant.

*Perdue chicken ad, as mistranslated abroad*

## Waffling

I'm not indecisive. Am I indecisive?

*Jim Siebel, Mayor of St Paul, Minnesota*

## Walking

Mr Asquith was like a drunken man walking along a straight line – the further he went the sooner he fell.

*Sir Edward Carson, famous Irish politician, and cross-examiner of Oscar Wilde*

## War

This is not a conventional war. We have to forget propriety.

*Colonel Robert A Koob, tentative head of jury in the Sergeant Charles E Hutto case. Hutto was accused of assault in the My Lai massacre during the Vietnam War*

If we let people see that kind of thing, there would never again be any war.

*Senior Pentagon official on reasons why United States military censored footage showing Iraqi soldiers sliced in two by US helicopter fire*

## War Movies

It made me nostalgic for arms talks and violence – it's a great dialectic.

*Former Secretary of State Alexander Haig, after seeing a blood and guts military movie,* The Package

## Watergate

What was Watergate? A little bugging!

*Richard Nixon*

I'm not going to comment from the White House on a third-rate burglary attempt.

*Ron Ziegler, Nixon press secretary*

I applaud President Nixon's comprehensive statement which clearly demonstrates again that the President was not involved with the Watergate matter.

*George Bush, prior to President Nixon's realization that maybe he was involved after all*

## Weapons

Fortunately, the rebels had no guns except pistols, cutlasses and pikes . . .

*Sir Boyle Roche, eighteenth-century MP from Tralee, in a letter to a friend*

I will ignore all ideas for new works on engines of war, the invention of which has reached its limits and for whose improvements I see no further hope.

*Sextus Julius Frontinus, first century AD Roman engineer*

## Weathermen

There is some possibility of showers tonight, according to Col J B Hersey, government meteorologist, although it is probable there will be no rain.

*Weather report in the* LA Express

## Wine

We are in a pretty mess; can get nothing to eat, and no wine to drink, except whiskey.

*Sir Boyle Roche, eighteenth-century MP from Tralee, and pre-eminent word mangler, in a letter to a friend about the poor state of Ireland*

## Wisdom

This is no time to pull the rug out in the middle of the stream.

*Representative Silvio Conte, of Massachusetts, during a heated Hose debate*

That's the most unheard-of thing I have ever heard of.

*Senator Joseph McCarthy, talking about a witness' testimony*

I do not feel that we should allow a shortage of funds to prevent cities from financing needed projects.

*Hubert Humphrey, Minnesota senator and former Vice-President*

I think that the free-enterprise system is absolutely too important to be left to the voluntary action of the marketplace.

*Congressman, Richard Kelly*

There are instances where it is in the best interests of the nation not to vote the will of the people.

*Ex-Speaker of the House, Thomas P (Tip) O'Neill Jr, on why Congress gave itself a pay raise without voting on the record for the raise*

I am ignorant of the Government's reasons, but I disapprove of them.

*James C Percy, citing an English MP during a heated parliamentary debate circa 1901*

## WIVES

I am glad to say that the first man to knock him down for doing such a thing was his own wife.

*A political campaign manager, talking about a man who didn't support his candidate*

The faithful watchdog or the good wife standing at the door to welcome the homecoming master with honest bark . . .

*Newspaper editor in Wisconsin, mid-1800s, infamous for word mangling*

## Women



Nobody can influence me. Nobody at all. And a woman still less.

*The ex-Shah of Iran*

I consider that women who are authors, lawyers and politicians are monsters.

*Pierre Auguste Renoir, French Impressionist painter and sculptor*

Literature cannot be the business of a woman's life, and it ought not to be. The more she is engaged in her proper duties, the less leisure she will have for it, even as her accomplishment and recreation. To those duties you have not yet been called, and when you are you will be less eager for celebrity.

*Robert Southey to Charlotte Brontë*

There has been no exclusion. We have simply excluded all the women.

*Nicolas Romanoff, descendant of last Czar of Russia, Nicholas II, explaining why no women were invited to a meeting to form a family foundation, as reported in* Fortune magazine

## Work

Work is the curse of the drinking classes.

*Revd William A Spooner*

## Working your way from the bottom up

My family worked for everything we had. We even have a deed from the King of England for property in South Carolina. Now these jerks come along and try to give it to the Communists.

*Martha Mitchell, wife of Attorney General John Mitchell*

## Writing

This is the best biography by me I have ever read.

*Orchestra leader Lawrence Welk, looking at his book on display at an American Booksellers Association convention*

I'm astounded by people who take eighteen years to write something. That's how long it took that guy to write Madame Bovary, and was that ever on the bestseller list?

*Sylvester Stallone*

You can't do it that way. You spoil the anti-climax.

*Michael Curtiz, film director, to a writer re-writing a scene*

. . . Writing, a reality not independent of human activity, is historically saturated and organized, embedded within the domain of productivity, and the word is 'the ideological phenomenon par excellence' . . .

*Myriam Diaz-Diocaretz, University of Utrecht, in her essay 'Sieving the matri-heritage of the sociotext', in* The Difference Within, *edited by E Meese and Alice Parker*

## Wrong

Caesar did never wrong save with just cause.

*William Shakespeare, in* Julius Caesar, *as noted in* The Handybook of Literary Curiosities, *by W Walsh, 1871*

## Yes-Men and Yes-Women

The President doesn't want any yes-men and yes-women around him. When he says no, we all say no.

*Elizabeth Dole, then assistant for public liaison to President Reagan, later Secretary of Labor under President Bush*

## About the authors

Ross and Kathryn Petras are writers and media junkies. When not collecting other people's stupidities, they collect their own in a computer file slugged 'Hall of Shame'.

## Acknowledgments

Thanks to everyone who helped make this book a reality, especially: Bruce Tracy, Robin Rue, Kris Dahl, Paul Bresnick, David Gernert and Susan Moldow – and, of course, to all the people who contributed their favourite stupidities.